Food's ready!

**74 delicious recipes
for everyone.**

HUNGRY? GREAT!

There are so many lunches, snacks and dinners in a lifetime, and we want them all to taste absolutely wonderful. In fact, we want all of life at home to be wonderful, from the entrance to the living room. This is our job, our mission – to create a better everyday life for you. In this book we come a little closer to everyday life and step into the kitchen, with all its pots and pans, to do some cooking. The result is 74 delicious new recipes* based on simple Swedish fare – meatballs, herring and salmon, pancakes, sandwiches and sweet things. The book is a journey of flavours, where you can try traditional Swedish meatballs with lingonberries and mashed potatoes, veggie balls in yellow curry, or chicken meatballs with acidic baked beetroot. There's herring as tasty tapas, and how about a pancake gateau with fresh berries? You'll have a chance to taste coriander salmon tartare, delightful shrimp sandwiches, and a generous smorgasbord with extra everything. And of course 'fika' – our Swedish word for coffee time with something sweet!

   Truly a book to fill you up – with food of course, but also with joy and inspiration!

David Johansson
Product Developer and Food Designer
IKEA Food Services

*All ingredients in **bold** can be found in the IKEA Swedish Food Market.

1. Wash your hands

2. Apron on

3. Favourite song on
and begin!

Herring

S

THE SECRETIVE SUPER-HERRING

There's something wonderfully mysterious about the herring. This silvery beauty swims in gigantic shoals with hundreds of millions of its little friends around the North Atlantic and the White Sea. Suddenly they all slam on the brakes, pop into a nice-looking bay, swim around and do a bit of shoaling. And then, just as suddenly, they're off again. It's a bit like when you serve different kinds of herring at the table; one minute they're there, the next they're gone, hoovered up by ravenous dinner guests. Mysterious!

Having said that, there's nothing particularly mysterious about eating herring – it's about the most Swedish thing you can do. They always taste good, on any ordinary day or a special occasion. And although the herring is quite a simple little fishy, it's an absolute must on the Swedish Christmas buffet or Midsummer smorgasbord. Acidic, salty or spiced – herring thrive in all kinds of flavours and any kind of pickle or marinade will bring out the best in them. Some people prefer to buy marinated herring, while others do their own marinating. There are all kinds of pickles and marinades. It's like with tomato sauce in Italy, every family has their own secret recipe.

Unpredictable and beautiful – meet the super-herring!

Butter, cheese and pickled herring
Serves 4

A simple classic Swedish starter, traditionally served with aquavit. If you can't get chives and dill, rocket and spring onions are good substitutes.

4 pieces soft thin bread (e.g. BRÖD TUNNBRÖD)
1 jar pickled herring (130 g drained weight) (e.g. SILL MATJES)
approx. 8 slices semi-hard cheese (e.g. OST HERRGÅRD)

BROWNED BUTTER WITH SOY SAUCE
50 g butter
2 tsp Japanese soy sauce

TO SERVE
Chives
Dill

1. Browned butter: Melt the butter in a saucepan over a medium heat. Stir and heat until golden brown. Pour into a small bowl and add the soy sauce. Set aside to cool.

2. Pre-heat the oven to 150°C. Cut the thin bread into smaller pieces and toast in the oven for 5-7 minutes until hard. Leave to cool.

3. Once the butter has cooled, whip into a creamy consistency. This takes about 5 minutes.

4. Spread a layer of soy butter onto the bread. Slice or cut the cheese, and place on the bread with the herring pieces.

5. Top with finely chopped chives and a few sprigs of dill.

Pickled herring cake

approx. 12 pieces

A herring cake may sound strange, but give it a try and you won't regret it. This pickled herring cake is great for a buffet and can be served whole or in pieces.

250 g rye bread (e.g. made from BRÖDMIX FLERKORN)
50 g butter
2 tsp runny honey

FILLING
3 gelatine leaves
2 jars pickled herring (260 g drained weight) (e.g. SILL MATJES)
1 small red onion
250 ml whipping cream
400 ml crème fraîche
Salt and white pepper
Dill
Chives

1. Brown the butter in a saucepan over a medium heat. Stir and heat until golden brown.

2. Crumb the rye bread by hand or in a food processor. Mix the crumbs with the melted butter and honey. Take a round springform cake tin, about 23 cm diameter, and line the base with baking paper. Press the breadcrumbs into the tin. Refrigerate for about 30 minutes until the bottom has hardened.

3. Filling: Place the gelatine leaves in a bowl of cold water. Save 3 tbsp of the liquid from the herring tin and set aside 8 pieces for garnish. Finely chop the rest of the herring, and the onion. Whip the cream in a bowl until hard. Mix into a consistent cream with the crème fraîche, herring, onion, salt and white pepper. Squeeze the water out of the gelatine leaves and melt in a saucepan over a low heat with 3 tbsp of herring liquid and about 2 tbsp of the herring mixture. Stir the gelatine mix into the bowl of herring mixture.

4. Pour the mixture into the tin. Spread it into an even layer and stand cold for 3-4 hours.

5. Serve the pickled herring cake garnished with herring, chopped dill and chives.

Pickled herring, egg and potatoes
Serves 4

*A light lunch or starter that's great when you have leftover boiled
potatoes. This recipe uses salad potatoes but any kind will work
as long as they're firm, quality potatoes.*

**1 jar pickled herring (130 g drained
  weight) (e.g. SILL MATJES)**
400 g salad potatoes
2 eggs
1 red onion
approx. 4 tbsp crème fraiche
Chives
Black pepper

RYE BREADCRUMBS
**1–2 slices rye bread (e.g. made from
  BRÖDMIX FLERKORN)**
Butter for frying

BROWNED BUTTER
50 g butter

1. Boil the potatoes, peel on. Hard boil the eggs.

2. Rye breadcrumbs: Dice the rye bread and fry
in butter.

3. Browned butter: Melt 50 g of butter in a
saucepan over a medium heat. Stir and heat until
golden brown.

4. Peel and thickly slice the potatoes and eggs.
Serve up on plates with the herring pieces. Sprinkle
on breadcrumbs, finely chopped red onion and
chopped chives.

5. Drizzle over browned butter, add a spoon of
crème fraîche and finish off with a little freshly ground
black pepper.

Tip:
A really fresh egg is harder to peel than a less fresh one.
Peeling is easier if the egg is cooled directly after boiling.

Herring tapas

Serves 4

Nice little dishes that are a great way to kick off a dinner or party.
You can use any kind of marinated herring, but the roast potatoes
go best with one in a creamy sauce.

MARINATED HERRING WITH ROAST POTATOES

1 jar marinated herring (130 g drained weight)
200 g potatoes
2 tbsp olive oil
approx. 1 tbsp capers
Salt and black pepper
Cress

APPLE AND CURRY HERRING

Crispbread (e.g. KNÄCKEBRÖD RÅG & KLI)
100 ml crème fraîche
1 tsp yellow curry powder
1/4 ml salt
1 apple, hard and acidic
approx. 2 tbsp chives
1 jar marinated herring (130 g drained weight)
Black pepper

1. Marinated herring with roast potatoes: Pre-heat the oven to 225°C. Cut the potatoes into slices about 1 1/5 cm thick. Lay onto a baking tray lined with baking paper and mix with olive oil, salt and pepper. Cook for about 25-30 minutes or until the potatoes are soft and nicely coloured. Remove from the oven and leave to cool. Place a piece of herring onto each piece of potato and garnish with capers and cut cress.

2. Apple and curry herring: Break the crispbread into smaller pieces. Mix the crème fraîche and curry powder into a consistent cream. Season with a little salt. Slice the apple and herring and fold into the curry cream. Place a dollop onto each piece of crispbread and top with chopped chives and freshly ground black pepper.

Salmon

ax

Whether you're a celebrity chef or are just starting to use your cooker, salmon is your best friend. That's because it's almost impossible to fail with this nice, fatty, healthy fish. There are almost endless ways of cooking its beautiful pink flesh. Eat it raw or raw spiced like gravlax, or salted or cold-smoked or hot-smoked or grilled or boiled or fried or poached or roasted or in a sandwich or in a salad. Season it with coconut or saffron or herbs or tandoori spices or mustard sauce or chilli or lemon – pretty much every-thing tastes great with salmon.

Salmon also has a handy little friend that will help you get the best out of your salmon dishes. It's called a thermometer. Salmon is tastiest if it's not cooked too long, so get a thermometer and you can keep an eye on when it's done.

Feeling down? Have salmon for dinner! The healthy omega 3 fatty acids in the fish have been shown to be good for your spirits. And if you want to be even happier – check out all our salmon recipes.

Cold-smoked salmon bake

Serves 4

A classic Swedish main course that's great mid-week or on a special occasion. If you make the bake in a bigger dish, you may need more potatoes and cream to fill it.

200 g cold-smoked salmon
500 g floury potatoes
1 onion
4 tbsp dill
350 ml single cream
3 eggs
Black pepper

1. Pre-heat the oven to 175°C.

2. Cut the potatoes and onion into thin slices. Whisk the eggs and cream together well. Season with pepper.

3. Alternate potatoes, salmon, onion and chopped dill into portion-sized dishes. Pour the egg and cream mix over the potatoes.

4. Cook for about 45 minutes or until the potatoes are soft and nicely coloured. Serve hot.

Tip:
This salmon bake is great served with melted butter.

Lemon risotto with cold-smoked salmon
Serves 4

A fresh, flavoursome risotto with crème fraîche instead of butter.
This risotto works best if the rice is still a bit al dente.

1 bunch green asparagus (250 g)
approx. 1 L chicken or vegetable stock
1 shallot
approx. 2 tbsp olive oil
400 ml risotto rice
200 ml white wine
100 ml crème fraîche
100 g semi-hard cheese + some to serve (e.g. OST PRÄST)
1/2 lemon, juice and zest
Salt and black pepper

TO SERVE
approx. 400 g cold-smoked salmon fillet

1. Rinse the asparagus and cut into pieces. Remove the bottom part.

2. Boil water and the stock in a separate pan.

3. Finely chop the shallot. Heat olive oil in a saucepan. Fry the onion without letting it colour.

4. Add the rice to the onion and cook for a further minute or so.

5. Add the wine and let it absorb.

6. Cover the rice with hot stock. Cook over a low heat.

7. As the stock absorbs, add more to cover the rice. Fold in the asparagus with the last lot of stock.

8. The rice will be ready after about 15-17 minutes.

9. Stir the crème fraîche, grated cheese and lemon zest into the rice. Season with lemon juice, salt and pepper.

10. Slice the salmon and serve with the risotto. Top off with shavings of cheese.

Salmon soup with green curry
Serves 4

An aromatic soup that's great with either fresh or frozen veg.
Curry paste can vary widely in strength so add it to taste.

4 salmon fillets, skin off (500 g)
approx. 1 tbsp green curry paste
1 onion
2 cloves garlic
1 tin coconut milk (400 ml)
300 ml water
1 tbsp fish sauce
300 g potatoes
300 g broccoli
50 g sugar snap peas
50 g green beans
1 lime, juice of
Oil for frying

TO SERVE
Fresh coriander

1. Heat the curry paste in a saucepan.

2. Shred the onion and finely chop the garlic. Stir into the curry paste and pour in a little oil. Fry over a medium heat for about 5 minutes.

3. Add the coconut milk, water and fish sauce and bring to the boil. Dice and add the potatoes. Simmer for about 10 minutes or until the potatoes are almost ready. Cut the broccoli into florets. Put them into the soup and simmer for a few minutes.

4. Cut the salmon into cubes of about 2 x 2 cm. Add to the soup a bit before serving, along with the green beans and sugar snap peas. Season with lime juice.

5. Garnish with fresh coriander and serve in deep bowls.

Tip:
Use leftover boiled potatoes if you have them.

Najad salmon with baked egg

Serves 4

A breakfast or lunch dish that can be served directly in nice portion-sized dishes. For more of an omelette dish, mix the eggs and the cream.

200 g Najad salmon (e.g. LAX NAJAD)
1 leek
300 ml fresh spinach
8 eggs
4 tbsp single cream
**approx. 200 ml semi-hard cheese,
    grated (e.g. OST PRÄST)**
Olive oil for frying
Salt and black pepper

1. Pre-heat the oven to 200°C.

2. Shred the leek and fry for a few minutes in olive oil without letting it colour.

3. Place the fried leek into four ovenproof portion-sized dishes. Then add the spinach, salmon slices, grated cheese and cream. Save a little spinach for the garnish.

4. Carefully break 2 eggs into each dish without breaking the yolks.

5. Put the dishes in the oven. Cook for 13-15 minutes or until the whites have set but the yolks are creamy.

7. Remove the dishes and garnish with chopped fresh spinach.

Tip:
Eggs last longer when stored pointy end down.

Salmon tartare with chilli and lime
Serves 4

A tartare is a dish where the ingredients are not heated. This salmon tartare is a fresh starter with Oriental flavours.

3 salmon fillets, skin off (375 g)
1/2 cucumber
2 spring onions
1 red chilli
2 tbsp Japanese soy sauce
1 tbsp sesame oil
1 lime, juice of

TO SERVE
approx. 70 g salad leaves
2 tbsp sesame seeds
about 50 ml fried onion (e.g. LÖK ROSTAD)
Fresh coriander

1. Cut the salmon into cubes of about 1/2 x 1/2 cm, thaw first if frozen. Place in a small bowl.

2. Cut the cucumber lengthways. Remove the watery middle and dice it. Finely chop the spring onions and chilli, and mix with the salmon pieces.

3. Mix the soy sauce, sesame oil and lime juice in a bowl. Carefully fold in with the salmon mixture.

4. Roast the sesame seeds in a dry frying pan, and leave to cool.

5. Place some salad leaves on four plates. Shape small salmon tartare portions with a spoon and serve onto the leaves. Garnish with the sesame seeds, fried onion and fresh coriander.

Tagliatelle with hot-smoked salmon and gremolata
Serves 4

A luxurious salmon dish you can prepare in no time. Gremolata is a mixture of parsley, garlic and lemon. In this version, it fries in the pan with a little hot chilli.

400 g tagliatelle
400 g hot-smoked salmon (e.g. LAX VARMRÖKT)

GREMOLATA
2 cloves garlic
1 red chilli
200 ml flat-leaf parsley
1 lemon, juice and zest
Olive oil for frying
Salt and black pepper

1. Cook the pasta as per the instructions on the packet.

2. Gremolata: Finely chop the garlic, chilli and parsley. Fry quickly in a hot pan with olive oil.

3. Place the pasta in the frying pan. Grate the lemon zest finely and mix it in. Season with olive oil, lemon juice, salt and pepper.

4. Break the hot-smoked salmon into pieces and place it on the pasta.

Tip:
Fresh herbs like parsley can be snipped with scissors as easily as cut with a knife.

Salt-baked salmon with potato & beetroot salad
Serves 4

Salmon baked in salt has a nice consistency and saltiness. Cooking time depends on how thick the salmon is. Using pre-cooked beetroot will save time.

500 g salmon, side of
approx. 400 g coarse salt
Black pepper

POTATO & BEETROOT SALAD
500 g potatoes
200 g beetroot
1 avocado

ELDERFLOWER VINAIGRETTE
3 tbsp vinegar (e.g. ÄPPELVINÄGER MED LINGON)
3 tbsp elderflower syrup (e.g. SAFT FLÄDER)
3 tbsp olive oil
1 shallot
50 ml capers
Salt and black pepper

1. Boil the potatoes and beetroot until soft (if using raw beetroot). Bear in mind that beetroot takes longer than potatoes.

2. Pre-heat the oven to 150°C. Place about a 1/2 cm thick layer of coarse salt into an ovenproof dish. Lay the salmon onto the salt skin down, and season with pepper. Cook in the oven for about 20 minutes or until the core temperature is 48-56°C.

3. Potato & beetroot salad: Mix the vinegar, elderflower syrup, olive oil, finely chopped shallot, capers, salt and pepper in a large bowl. Cut the potatoes, beetroot and avocado into wedges. Fold into the bowl with the vinaigrette. Mix well.

4. Serve the salmon with the potato & beetroot salad.

Salmon with sweet potato & lentil salad
Serves 4

Beluga lentils are tasty, visually appealing and don't need to be soaked before cooking. You can also use pre-cooked lentils or some other kind of lentils.

4 salmon fillets, skin off (500 g)
1 tsp dried chilli
approx. 1 tsp salt
Oil for frying

SWEET POTATO & LENTIL SALAD
200 ml dried beluga lentils
400 g sweet potatoes
1 red chilli
1 tbsp olive oil
approx. 80 g rocket
150 g feta cheese
Salt

ORANGE DRESSING
3 tbsp butter
1 shallot
1 orange, juice and zest
2 tbsp vinegar (e.g. ÄPPELVINÄGER MED LINGON)

1. Pre-heat the oven to 200°C.

2. Sweet potato & lentil salad: Cook the lentils as per the instructions on the packet. Drain them well, otherwise the salad can be too watery. Peel the sweet potatoes and cut into cubes of about 2 x 2 cm. Finely chop the chilli. Place the sweet potatoes and chilli on a baking tray and mix with olive oil and salt. Roast until the sweet potatoes are soft, about 20 minutes. Mix the lentils, roast sweet potatoes, rocket and feta pieces in a large bowl.

3. Orange dressing: Melt the butter while stirring, until golden brown. Add the finely chopped shallot. Grate the zest of half an orange and add the juice of a whole one. Add vinegar and remove the pan from the heat.

4. Rub the salmon fillets with chilli and salt. Fry over a medium heat for about 6-7 minutes on one side and 1-2 minutes on the other. The salmon is ready when the core temperature is 48-56°C.

5. Serve the salmon with the lentil salad and orange dressing.

Salmon parcels with vegetables
Serves 4

A complete all-in-one meal that looks after itself in the oven.
The butter jus is an added bonus. The veg can vary, use whatever
you have at home.

4 salmon fillets, skin off (500 g)
500 g floury potatoes
1 leek
1 head of fennel
8 cherry tomatoes
8 sugar snap peas
approx. 50 g butter
1 clove garlic
4 tbsp capers
1 tsp thyme
4 tbsp parsley + a little to garnish
1 lemon, juice and zest
Salt and black pepper

1. Pre-heat the oven to 175°C.

2. Peel the potatoes and cut into cubes of about 1 x 1 cm. Slice the leek and fennel.

3. Cut out rectangles of baking paper about 25 x 40 cm. Place potatoes, veg and salmon onto one half of the rectangle. Top off with a spoon of butter, grated garlic, capers, thyme, chopped parsley, lemon juice and a little grated lemon zest. Season with salt and pepper. Fold the empty half over, roll the sides up and pinch them together.

4. Place the parcels on a baking tray. Cook in the oven for about 20 minutes or until the potatoes are soft and the salmon cooked through.

5. Serve straight from the parcels.

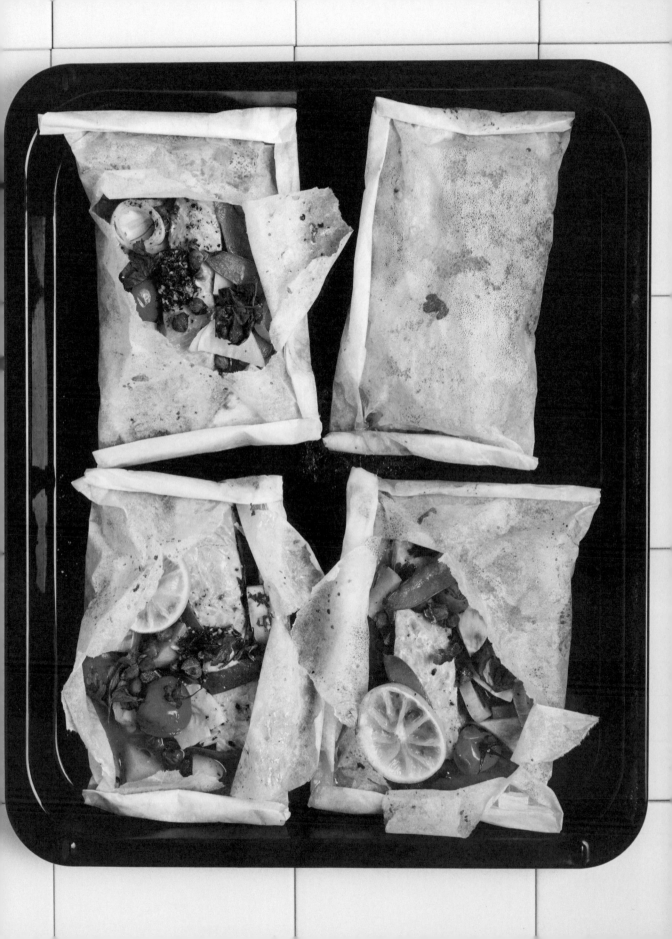

Salmon soup with saffron and thyme aioli
Serves 4

*A warming soup with a wonderful flavour of saffron, fennel and
orange. You can use fresh or dried thyme for the aioli.*

4 salmon fillets, skin off (500 g)
500 g shrimps, shells on
1 onion
3 cloves garlic
1 tbsp olive oil
500 g potatoes
1 carrot
1 head of fennel
1 L water + 3 fish stock cubes
1 tin chopped tomatoes (400 g)
200 ml white wine
1 tsp thyme
½ g saffron
1/2 orange, juice of
Salt and black pepper
Parsley

THYME AIOLI
100 ml mayonnaise
1 clove garlic
1/2 tsp thyme
Salt

1. Defrost and peel the shrimps.

2. Thyme aioli: Mix together the mayonnaise, finely
chopped garlic and thyme. Season with salt.

3. Chop the onion and garlic. Fry in a saucepan
over a medium heat until soft and transparent. Cut
the potatoes, carrot and fennel into cubes of about
2 x 2 cm. Add to the saucepan.

4. Pour on the water and add the stock cubes,
chopped tomatoes, white wine, thyme and saffron.
Simmer for around 20 minutes.

5. Season the soup with the orange juice, salt and
pepper.

6. Cut the salmon fillets into cubes of about 3 x 3 cm.
Add to the soup and simmer for a couple of minutes
before serving.

7. Serve the soup with shrimps, chopped fresh
parsley and aioli.

Salmon with teriyaki sauce and pak choi
Serves 4

Salmon rubbed with sugar or honey looks extra tasty when fried.
Pak choi is a kind of cabbage, but you can use broccoli or green
beans instead.

4 salmon fillets, skin off (500 g)
4 ml sugar or honey
1 tsp chilli
1 tsp salt

TERIYAKI SAUCE
2 tbsp vinegar (e.g. ÄPPELVINÄGER
   MED LINGON)
3 tbsp Japanese soy sauce
2 tbsp neutral oil
2 tbsp sesame oil
3 tbsp sweet chilli sauce
2 cloves garlic
2 tsp fresh ginger, grated

FRIED PAK CHOI
2 pak choi
1 tbsp neutral oil
Salt

TO SERVE
4 portions jasmine rice
2 tbsp sesame seeds

1. Pre-heat the oven to 150°C.

2. Boil the rice as per the instructions on the packet.

3. Teriyaki sauce: Mix the vinegar, soy sauce, oil, sesame oil and sweet chilli sauce in a bowl. Stir in the finely chopped or grated garlic and ginger. Leave to stand until time to serve.

4. Rub the salmon with salt, sugar (or honey) and chilli. Fry one side in a hot oiled frying pan for about 10 seconds, or until it turns a nice colour. Place in an ovenproof dish, fried side up. Finish off in the oven for about 7 minutes or until the core temperature is 48-56°C.

5. Fried pak choi: Cut the pak choi into two or four. Season with salt and fry or wok in oil until it has softened but is still a bit al dente.

6. Serve the salmon with rice, pak choi and teriyaki sauce. Garnish with sesame seeds.

Tandoori-spiced salmon with fennel raita
Serves 4

*A colourful dish. Salmon and tandoori spices go really well together.
In this recipe the raita, which is a kind of yogurt sauce, has the lovely
added flavour of fresh fennel.*

4 salmon fillets, skin off (500 g)
approx. 4 tsp tandoori spice
Salt

FENNEL RAITA
1 small cucumber
1 small head of fennel
1 small red onion
1 red chilli
200 ml yoghurt, 10% fat
1/2 tsp ground cumin
2 tbsp mint
Salt and black pepper

TO SERVE
4 portions jasmine rice
approx. 100 g mixed green salad
1 carrot

1. Boil the rice as per the instructions on the packet.

2. Pre-heat the oven to 150°C.

3. Rub the salmon fillets with salt and tandoori spice. Fry one side in a hot oiled frying pan for about 10 seconds, or until it turns a nice colour. Place in an ovenproof dish, fried side up. Finish off in the oven for about 7 minutes or until the core temperature is 48-56°C.

4. Fennel raita: Cut the cucumber lengthways. Remove the watery middle. Dice it and the fennel. Place in a bowl with finely chopped red onion and chilli. Stir in the yoghurt, cumin and finely chopped mint. Season with salt and pepper.

5. Peel and slice the carrot with a potato peeler and mix with the salad leaves.

6. Serve the salmon with rice, fennel raita and salad.

Sesame-coated salmon with noodle salad
Serves 4

Noodle salad is a quick, tasty accompaniment to salmon.
You can replace the peanuts with sunflower seeds toasted
in sesame oil and salt.

4 salmon fillets, skin off (500 g)
1 tsp salt
1/2 tsp cayenne pepper
50 ml sesame seeds
Oil for frying

NOODLE SALAD
4 portions glass noodles
2 spring onions
1/2 cucumber
2 carrots
50 ml mint
100 ml fresh coriander

DRESSING
1 tbsp vinegar (e.g. ÄPPELVINÄGER
  MED LINGON)
4 tbsp fish sauce
1 lime, juice of (approx. 2 tbsp)
2 tbsp sugar
1 red chilli
1 clove garlic
Chilli paste, e.g. sambal oelek

TO SERVE
100 ml peanuts

1. Pre-heat the oven to 150°C.

2. Noodle salad: Cook the noodles as per the instructions on the packet. When done, rinse under cold water to cool. Drain and place in a bowl with the spring onion cut into strips, sliced cucumber and sliced carrot. Save a few sprigs of mint and coriander for garnish, and chop the rest into the salad.

3. Dressing: Mix the vinegar, fish sauce, lime juice and sugar. Stir until the sugar dissolves. Add finely chopped chilli and garlic. Add chilli paste if you prefer a hotter dish. Pour the dressing over the noodles and veg and mix well.

4. Cut each salmon piece into two. Rub in salt and coat in a mixture of sesame seeds and cayenne pepper. Fry over a medium heat in a little oil for about 6-7 minutes on one side and 1-2 minutes on the other. The salmon is ready when the core temperature is 48-56°C.

5. Serve up on plates with the noodles. Sprinkle over peanuts, fresh coriander and mint.

Salmon and potato fry with caviar sauce
Serves 4

*This is a tasty fried dish and a great way to use salmon. Feel free
to try replacing some of the potato with other root vegetables like
celeriac or parsnip.*

**400 g hot-smoked salmon (e.g. LAX
    VARMRÖKT)**
750 g firm potatoes
1 courgette
1 leek
approx. 4 tbsp dill + a little to garnish
Butter for frying
Salt and black pepper

CAVIAR SAUCE
200 ml crème fraîche
4 tbsp caviar

TO SERVE
4 egg yolks

1. Dice the potatoes and courgettes. Slice the leek.

2. Fry the potatoes in butter over a medium heat
until they start to soften. Add the courgette and fry
until soft. Add the leek and fry until it starts to brown.
Season with salt and pepper. Remove the pan from
the heat.

3. Caviar sauce: Mix the crème fraîche and caviar
in a bowl.

4. Set aside a few nice sprigs of dill to garnish.
Coarsely chop the rest and add it to the potatoes.
Break the salmon into pieces and fold in carefully.
Break the eggs and separate the yolks and whites.
Place each yolk in a small glass.

5. Serve the fry with caviar sauce, a few sprigs of
dill and raw egg yolk.

Tip:
Use the egg whites for meringue or mousse.
You can also freeze them, they last for ages.

Salmon burger with celery coleslaw
Serves 4

The salmon's juiciness makes it ideal for burgers. You can season the salmon mince in all kinds of ways, e.g. with chilli, ginger, dill and capers. Instead of panko you can use ordinary breadcrumbs or desiccated coconut.

4 salmon fillets, skin off (500 g)
2 tbsp mayonnaise
approx. 1 tbsp lemon juice
100 ml panko + for coating
Salt and black pepper
Oil for frying

CELERY COLESLAW
3 tbsp horseradish sauce
50 ml mayonnaise
approx. 200 g cabbage
2 stalks celery
Salt and black pepper

TO SERVE
4 bread rolls
1 head of cos lettuce
1 green apple
4 cherry tomatoes
1 red onion
4 sprigs of basil
4 tbsp mayonnaise

1. Finely chop the salmon and mix it with the mayo, lemon juice, panko, salt and pepper.

2. Celery coleslaw: Mix the horseradish sauce and mayo in a bowl. Shred the cabbage and celery. Fold into the horseradish mayo. Season with salt and pepper.

3. Shape the salmon mince into burgers and turn in a plate of panko. Fry the burgers for a few minutes either side until golden brown.

4. Cut the rolls and fry a little on each side. Add lettuce, sliced apple, coleslaw, the salmon burger, sliced tomato and red onion. Top with a little mayo, a sprig of basil and freshly ground black pepper.

Salmon with potato & fennel gratin
Serves 4

This creamy fennel gratin is an amazing accompaniment to salmon.
If you make the gratin in a large dish, you may need to adjust the
amount of wine, cream and potatoes.

4 salmon fillets, skin off (500 g)
Salt and black pepper
Oil for frying

POTATO & FENNEL GRATIN
approx. 400 g potatoes
1 head of fennel
1 onion
2 cloves garlic
approx. 3 tsp thyme
**approx. 200 ml semi-hard cheese,
grated (e.g. OST PRÄST)**
100 ml white wine
300 ml single cream
Salt and black pepper

TO SERVE
80 g green salad leaves
approx. 1/2 lemon

1. Pre-heat the oven to 225°C.

2. Potato & fennel gratin: Slice the potatoes, fennel, onion and garlic. Place the veg in a saucepan along with the cream, wine, thyme, salt and black pepper. Bring to the boil and simmer until softened slightly.

3. Place the boiled veg and cream into four portion-sized dishes or one large one. Top with the cheese. Cook in the oven for about 15 minutes or until the potatoes brown nicely.

4. Season the salmon with salt and pepper. Fry over a medium heat in a little oil for about 6-7 minutes on one side and 1-2 minutes on the other. The salmon is ready when the core temperature is 48-56°C.

5. Serve the salmon with the potato & fennel gratin, green salad and a wedge of lemon.

Lax **Salmon**

Salmon with red cabbage salad
Serves 4

*Mustard and horseradish are great flavours alongside salmon.
Red cabbage makes this a colourful dish, but any other kind is fine
such as ordinary cabbage, spring greens or kale.*

4 salmon fillets, skin off (500 g)
Salt and black pepper
Oil for frying

MUSTARD-TOSSED POTATOES
500 g potatoes
1 tbsp olive oil
**1 tbsp vinegar (e.g. ÄPPELVINÄGER
    MED LINGON)**
**1 tbsp whole-grain mustard
    (e.g. SENAP GROV)**
1 tbsp horseradish sauce
2 tbsp mayonnaise
1 clove garlic
1 1/2 tbsp chopped chives
Salt and black pepper

RED CABBAGE SALAD
200 g red cabbage
**2 tbsp vinegar (e.g. ÄPPELVINÄGER
    MED LINGON)**
**2 tbsp lingonberry syrup (e.g. SAFT
    LINGON)**
2 tbsp olive oil
50 ml pumpkin seeds
Salt and black pepper

1. Pre-heat the oven to 200°C.

2. Mustard-tossed potatoes: Cut the potatoes in halves or quarters depending on size. Mix with olive oil and place in an ovenproof dish. Cook in the oven for about 30 minutes or until the potatoes are soft. Reduce the heat to 150°C.

3. Mix the vinegar, mustard, horseradish sauce and mayo in a bowl. Stir in finely chopped garlic. Season with salt and pepper. Mix with the hot potatoes.

4. Red cabbage salad: Mix the vinegar, lingonberry syrup and olive oil in a bowl. Shred the red cabbage and fold into the dressing with the pumpkin seeds. Mix well. Season with salt and pepper.

5. Salt and pepper the salmon on both sides. Fry one side in a hot oiled frying pan for about 10 seconds, or until it turns a nice colour. Place in an ovenproof dish, fried side up. Finish off in the oven for about 7 minutes or until the core temperature is 48-56°C.

6. Serve the salmon with the mustard-tossed potatoes and red cabbage salad. Garnish with chopped chives and freshly ground black pepper.

Salmon with summer vegetables and lemon sauce
Serves 4

*A fresh, summery dish with lovely early vegetables. Fresh thyme can
be replaced with pea shoots.*

4 salmon fillets, skin off (500 g)
4 carrots
300 g sugar snap peas
1 leek
Olive oil for frying
Salt and black pepper
Fresh thyme

LEMON SAUCE
**1 pack lemon sauce (e.g. SÅS CITRON
& DILL)**
Black pepper

1. Pre-heat the oven to 150°C.

2. Salt and pepper the salmon on both sides. Fry one
side in a hot oiled frying pan for about 10 seconds,
or until it turns a nice colour. Place in an ovenproof
dish, fried side up. Finish off in the oven for about
7 minutes or until the core temperature is 48-56°C.

3. Cut the vegetables thinly. Fry quickly in olive oil.
Season with salt.

4. Lemon sauce: Heat the sauce carefully in a
saucepan.

5. Place the salmon and veg on plates. Garnish with
fresh thyme.

6. Serve with the lemon sauce and freshly ground
black pepper.

Tip:
*Fish should be defrosted slowly in the fridge
to preserve the quality of the meat.*

Fried salmon with cauliflower purée
Serves 4

*Cauliflower purée is a creamy, tasty accompaniment to salmon.
Drain the cauliflower thoroughly before blending it, otherwise
the purée can easily be too runny.*

4 salmon fillets, skin off (500 g)
Salt and black pepper
Oil for frying

CAULIFLOWER PURÉE
900 g cauliflower (1–2 heads)
1 onion
approx. 6 tbsp crème fraîche
**100 ml semi-hard cheese, grated
(e.g. OST PRÄST)**
Salt and black pepper

CELERY SALAD
4–6 stalks celery
**1 tbsp vinegar (e.g. ÄPPELVINÄGER
MED LINGON)**
1 tbsp olive oil
50 ml sunflower seeds
Parsley
Salt and black pepper

1. Cauliflower purée: Cut the onion and cauliflower into smaller pieces. Boil them in salted water for about 5 minutes until soft. Drain well. Blend the cauliflower and onion with the crème fraîche and grated cheese into a smooth purée. Season with salt and pepper.

2. Celery salad: Slice the celery stalks lengthways with a potato peeler. Place in cold water a while to crisp them up. Leave to dry on kitchen paper. Mix the vinegar and olive oil in a salad bowl. Season with salt and pepper. Toast the sunflower seeds in a frying pan until nicely browned. Place the celery in the salad bowl. Mix everything well with the sunflower seeds.

3. Salt and pepper the salmon on both sides. Fry over a medium heat in a little oil for about 6-7 minutes on one side and 1-2 minutes on the other. The salmon is ready when the core temperature is 48-56°C.

4. Serve the salmon fillets with the cauliflower purée and celery salad. Garnish with chopped parsley and freshly ground black pepper.

Hot-smoked salmon salad with pear vinaigrette
Serves 4

*An easy, appealing salad that works as a main course. You can speed
up preparation by cutting the celeriac into large pieces and roasting
them for about 20 minutes.*

**400 g hot-smoked salmon (e.g. LAX
  VARMRÖKT)**
150–200 g mixed salad leaves
1 pomegranate
200 ml walnuts
1 large pear

BAKED WHOLE CELERIAC
1 celeriac
Olive oil
Salt

PEAR VINAIGRETTE
50 g raw sugar
**200 ml vinegar (e.g. ÄPPELVINÄGER
  MED LINGON)**
1 pear
1 clove garlic
1 lemon, juice of
100 ml olive oil
1 tsp dried thyme
Salt and black pepper

1. Baked whole celeriac: Rub the celeriac with oil
and salt. Roast at 175°C for 60-90 minutes or until
it's soft all the way through.

2. Toast the walnuts in a dry frying pan.

3. Pear vinaigrette: Bring the vinegar and sugar to the
boil in a saucepan. Stir in peeled, coarsely chopped
pear and garlic. Simmer for 5-7 minutes or so.
Remove the vinegar saucepan from the heat. Add the
lemon juice, olive oil and thyme. Blend the vinaigrette
with a stick blender. Season with salt and pepper.
Pour into a glass jar and store cool.

4. Place some salad leaves on four plates. Then add
the hot-smoked salmon, pomegranate seeds, toasted
walnuts, and the celeriac and pear cut into pieces.
Serve with the pear vinaigrette.

Gravlax with poached egg and herb oil

Serves 4

*A luxurious breakfast or a light lunch. Use an egg timer and
make sure the eggs are as fresh as possible to get the poach right.
Cold-smoked salmon can be used instead of gravlax.*

**4 slices soft wheat bread (e.g. BRÖD
    MJUKKAKA)**
200 g gravlax

HERB OIL
2 tbsp dill + a little to garnish
2 tbsp chives + a little to garnish
75 ml neutral oil
approx. 1 tsp lemon juice
Salt and black pepper

POACHED EGG
4 eggs
1 tbsp white wine vinegar
1 tsp salt

1. Herb oil: Chop the dill and chives. Save a little for garnish. Blend the oil, dill, chives and lemon juice in a bowl. Season with salt and pepper.

2. Poached egg: Bring water, vinegar and salt to the boil in a saucepan. Reduce the heat. The water should only simmer when the eggs are tipped in. Stir up a whirlpool with a perforated ladle. Break one egg at a time into a cup and carefully tip it into the whirlpool. After the required cooking time, lift the eggs out with a perforated ladle. Drain on kitchen paper.

3. Place the bread slices onto plates. Add salmon slices, poached eggs, herb oil and chopped herbs.

EGG COOKING TIMES
about 3 minutes for a runny yolk
about 4–5 minutes for a creamy yolk
about 6 minutes for a firm yolk

Salmon and kale salad with lemon
Serves 4

Here the salmon is served with a fresh salad of lightly fried kale, lemon, grated cheese and toasted pine nuts. Serve with bread for a more filling dish.

4 salmon fillets, skin off (500 g)
Salt and black pepper
Oil for frying

KALE SALAD
approx. 300 g kale
2 tbsp olive oil
1 lemon, juice of
**100 ml semi-hard cheese, grated
   (e.g. OST PRÄST)**
100 ml pine kernels
Salt and black pepper

1. Kale salad: Trim and shred the kale. Fry it in olive oil in a frying pan for a few minutes until it softens slightly. Mix in the pressed lemon and grated cheese.

2. Season the salmon with salt and pepper on both sides. Fry over a medium heat in a little oil for about 6-7 minutes on one side and 1-2 minutes on the other. The salmon is ready when the core temperature is 48-56°C.

3. Toast the pine nuts in a frying pan. Fold into the kale salad. Season with salt and pepper.

4. Serve the salmon on a bed of kale salad.

Tip:
Before pressing the lemon, roll it warm in the palm of your hand or heat in the microwave for 10-20 seconds. This will give you more juice.

Bibimbap with salmon and fried egg
Serves 4

*Bibimbap is a Korean dish that includes rice, hot chilli sauce
and mixed vegetables.*

4 salmon fillets, skin off (500 g)
Salt and black pepper

CHILLI-MARINATED CUCUMBER
1 batch pickled cucumber, see page 84
    (Swedish meatball platter)
1 tsp chilli paste

BIBIMBAP SAUCE
1 tbsp sesame seeds
1 clove garlic
2 tbsp chilli paste, e.g. sambal oelek
2 tbsp sesame oil
2 tbsp honey
**1 tsp vinegar (e.g. ÄPPELVINÄGER
    MED LINGON)**

QUICK-FRIED SPINACH
1 clove garlic
1 tbsp sesame oil
300 g fresh spinach
1 tbsp Japanese soy sauce
1 tbsp sesame seeds

TO SERVE
4 portions basmati rice
4 eggs
approx. 100 ml kimchi (bought)

1. Pre-heat the oven to 150°C. Boil the rice as per the instructions on the packet.

2. Chilli-marinated cucumber: Make the pickled cucumber as per the recipe on page 84, but instead of parsley use chilli paste.

3. Bibimbap sauce: Finely chop the garlic and stir it in with the sesame seeds, chilli paste, sesame oil, honey and vinegar.

4. Season the salmon with salt and pepper on both sides. Fry one side in a hot oiled frying pan for about 10 seconds, or until it turns a nice colour. Place in an ovenproof dish, fried side up. Finish off in the oven for about 7 minutes or until the core temperature is 48-56°C.

5. Quick-fried spinach: Fry the finely chopped garlic and spinach quickly in sesame oil. Add the soy sauce and sesame seeds.

6. Fry the eggs on one side.

7. Serve the salmon with the accompaniments.

Cold-smoked salmon with brussels sprout salad
Serves 4

A salad packed with flavours: smoked salmon, sweet cranberries,
acidic lingonberry vinaigrette and crispy fresh leaves. If brussels
aren't in season, use radicchio or endives instead.

200 g cold-smoked salmon fillet

BRUSSELS SPROUT SALAD
approx. 200 g brussels sprouts
3 stalks celery
approx. 150 g rocket
approx. 100 ml dried cranberries
200 ml semi-hard cheese, grated
  (e.g. OST HERRGÅRD)
150 ml pumpkin seeds

LINGONBERRY VINAIGRETTE
3 tbsp lingonberry jam (e.g. SYLT
  LINGON)
2 tbsp vinegar (e.g. ÄPPELVINÄGER
  MED LINGON)
1/2 lemon, juice of
3 tbsp olive oil
Salt and black pepper

1. Brussels sprout salad: Finely shred the brussels and celery with a knife or mandolin. Save a few whole sprout leaves for decoration. Place in a large bowl. Mix in the rocket, cranberries and grated cheese.

2. Toast the pumpkin seeds in a frying pan until nicely browned. Fold into the salad.

3. Lingonberry vinaigrette: Mix all the ingredients together. Pour the vinaigrette over the salad and mix well.

4. Serve with sliced cold-smoked salmon and freshly ground black pepper.

Tip:
The edges of old cheeses can be grated and frozen. They're
great to have handy for gratin dishes and quiches.

Salmon fishcakes and mango salsa
Serves 4

These fish cakes are dead easy to make and taste great. The Japanese panko breadcrumbs make for a light, crispy coating, but regular breadcrumbs are fine too.

4 salmon fillets, skin off (500 g)
2 tbsp fresh ginger
1 red chilli
1/2 lime, juice and zest
1 tbsp fish sauce
1/2 tsp salt
approx. 200 ml panko
Oil for frying

MANGO SALSA
1 mango
1 red onion
1 red chilli
1/2 lime, juice and zest
2 tbsp fish sauce
Mint
Fresh coriander

TO SERVE
150 g green salad leaves, e.g. lamb's
   lettuce

1. Chop or blend the salmon finely in a food processor. Place in a bowl. Add the grated ginger and finely chopped chilli, along with the pressed juice and zest of half a lime. Stir in the fish sauce and salt. Set to one side.

2. Mango salsa: In a bowl, mix diced mango, finely chopped red onion and finely chopped chili with the juice and zest of the other half of lime. Add fish sauce, and chopped mint and coriander. Mix. Leave to stand until time to serve.

3. Roll the salmon mix into balls with about 50 ml in each. Press the balls slightly and turn in a bowl of panko. Fry the breaded fish cakes for a few minutes either side until golden brown.

4. Serve the fish cakes with the mango salsa on a bed of green salad leaves, mint and fresh coriander.

Smoky chilli salmon and salad with pan-toasted corn
Serves 4

The chipotle, smoked chilli, gives the salmon a strong, slightly smoky flavour. If you can't get chipotle, use smoked sweet pepper instead.

4 salmon fillets, skin off (500 g)
2 tsp dried chipotle
1 tsp sugar
1 tsp salt
Oil for frying

SALAD WITH PAN-TOASTED CORN
approx. 1 1/2 tbsp neutral oil
800 ml sweet corn (frozen or tinned)
2 cloves garlic
3 spring onions
1 1/2 tsp chilli paste, e.g. sambal oelek
3 tbsp mayonnaise
approx. 150 ml semi-hard cheese, grated (e.g. OST HERRGÅRD)
100 ml fresh coriander + a little to garnish
approx. 1/2 lime, juice of
1 avocado
Salt

1. Pre-heat the oven to 150°C.

2. Salad with pan-toasted corn: Toast the corn in a frying pan until it browns. Add the finely chopped garlic, sliced spring onions and chilli paste. Fry a further minute or so. Transfer everything to a bowl and fold in the mayo, grated cheese and coarsely chopped coriander. Season with salt and lime juice and possibly a bit more chilli paste.

3. Rub the salmon with salt, sugar and chipotle. Fry one side in a hot oiled frying pan for about 10 seconds, or until it turns a nice golden brown. Place in an ovenproof dish, fried side up. Finish off in the oven for about 7 minutes or until the core temperature is 48-56°C.

4. Serve the salmon and corn salad onto plates. Garnish with diced avocado and fresh coriander.

Cold-smoked salmon with preserved vegetables
Serves 4

*Quick-preserved vegetables make a crispy accompaniment to
cold-smoked salmon. Use cauliflower, carrots and leeks, for example.
The veg will keep for about two weeks in the fridge.*

**approx. 400 g cold-smoked salmon
    fillet**
750 g potatoes, e.g. salad potatoes

PRESERVED VEGETABLES
**200 ml vinegar (e.g. ÄPPELVINÄGER
    MED LINGON)**
100 ml water
2 tbsp sugar
1 ml salt
approx. 250 g mixed vegetables

MUSTARD CREAM
**2 tbsp whole-grain mustard
    (e.g. SENAP GROV)**
100 ml crème fraîche
Salt and black pepper

TO SERVE
50 g butter
Dill

1. Boil the potatoes, peel on.

2. Quick-preserved vegetables: Mix together all
the ingredients for the preserving vinegar in a bowl.
Stir until the sugar dissolves. Coarsely chop the veg
and place in the vinegar. Leave to stand until time
to serve.

3. Mustard cream: Mix the mustard and crème
fraîche. Season with salt and pepper.

4. Melt the butter. Cut the cold-smoked salmon
into four portions.

5. Peel the potatoes if the peel is thick. Place onto
plates. Drizzle the melted butter over and add
the salmon.

6. Serve with preserved vegetables, mustard cream
and a few sprigs of dill.

Tip:
*Ideally make the preserved veg a day
before. Leaving them to pickle overnight
just makes them tastier.*

Kött

Meatballs

bullar

HEY MEATBALL!

The meatball must be just about the cutest little piece of everyday food, and it comes in a wide range of varieties all over the world. Small, round and generally pleasant, it has the ability to taste good in any situation. Meatballs are rarely any trouble, and they're a very useful friend to have in the freezer. But despite its unassuming nature, it can be really adventurous too. It's just as happy in an Indian curry or alongside a fine, garlicky aubergine, as it is next to a creamy houmous. The traditional Swedish way to eat it is with a mild cream sauce, mashed potatoes, sweet lingonberries and acidic pickled gherkins.

Yes, the meatball is something of a chameleon in the kitchen as it goes so well with so many different flavours. The meatball also has two friendly cousins: the chicken meatball and the veggie ball, and you'll meet them here too.

Read on to discover some new sides to our little Swedish meatball. We hope the recipes will inspire you to step inside a world of exciting flavours. And remember, in the company of a nice little meatball, nothing can go wrong.

Köttbullar

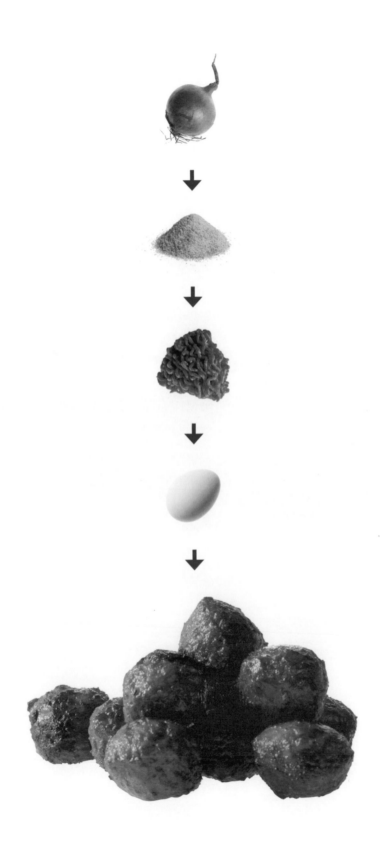

Swedish meatball platter
Serves 4

In Sweden, meatballs are traditionally served with mashed potatoes, lingonberry jam, cream sauce and pickled cucumber. Ideally make the cucumber a day in advance to increase the flavour.

32 meatballs (e.g. KÖTTBULLAR)

PICKLED CUCUMBER
1/2 cucumber, approx. 125 g
3 tbsp white wine vinegar
100 ml warm water
1 tbsp sugar
1 ml salt
1 tbsp parsley

MASHED POTATOES
600 g mashed potatoes (e.g. POTATIS-MOS)

CREAM SAUCE
400 ml cream sauce (e.g. GRÄDDSÅS)

TO SERVE
200 ml lingonberry jam (e.g. SYLT LINGON)

1. Meatballs: Pre-heat the oven to 225°C. Place the frozen meatballs on a baking tray. Heat in the middle of the oven for about 15 minutes.

2. Pickled cucumber: Slice the cucumber thinly. Mix the vinegar, water, sugar and salt until the sugar and salt dissolve. Add the cucumber. Leave to stand cool until time to serve. Garnish with a little parsley.

3. Mashed potatoes: Prepare as per the instructions on the packet.

4. Cream sauce: Prepare as per the instructions on the packet.

5. Serve the meatballs with mashed potatoes, cream sauce, pickled cucumber and a spoonful of lingonberry jam.

Tip:
Add more flavour to the mash with grated cheese, chives and chopped parsley. Fried mushrooms or fried onions are great for adding to the sauce.

Veggie balls with tabbouleh
Serves 4

*An aromatic dish inspired by the falafel platter.
Quinoa can be used instead of bulgur.*

32 veggie balls (e.g. GRÖNSAKSBULLAR)
approx. 1 tsp cumin
Olive oil for the baking tray

TABBOULEH
100 ml bulgur
3 tomatoes
300 ml flat-leaf parsley
100 ml mint leaves
1 spring onion
1 ml ground cinnamon
1/2 lemon, juice of
1 tbsp olive oil
Salt and black pepper

HOUMOUS
1 tin chickpeas, drained (approx. 300 ml)
50 ml olive oil
1 tbsp tahini
approx. 1 tbsp water
1 clove garlic
1 ml cumin
1 ml cayenne pepper
approx. 1 tbsp lemon juice
Salt

TO SERVE
**4 pieces soft thin bread (e.g. BRÖD
   TUNNBRÖD)**

1. Tabbouleh: Boil the bulgur as per the instructions on the packet and leave to cool. Scoop out the tomatoes, dice and place in a large bowl. Chop the parsley, mint and spring onion. Pour off the excess water from the tomatoes. Mix in the herbs, spring onion, spices and olive oil. Season with lemon juice, salt and pepper.

2. Pre-heat the oven to 180°C. Place the frozen veggie balls onto a lightly oiled baking tray. Season with cumin and shake the tray. Heat in the middle of the oven for about 20 minutes.

3. Houmous: Put all the ingredients in a bowl. Blend into a smooth paste using a stick blender. Season to taste with spices, tahini, lemon and salt. If the mix is too stiff, add more water.

4. Place the tabbouleh, houmous and veggie balls on four plates and serve with the thin bread.

Veggie balls with roast cherry tomatoes
Serves 4

Cherry tomatoes roasted in the oven take on a lovely flavour and almost become a spice. Bulgur can be replaced by whole-grain wheat, oat groats, rice or quinoa.

32 veggie balls (e.g. GRÖNSAKSBULLAR)
Oil for the baking tray

ROAST CHERRY TOMATOES
400 g cherry tomatoes
1 tsp thyme
1 clove garlic
2 tbsp olive oil
Salt and black pepper

ELDERFLOWER VINAIGRETTE
3 tbsp vinegar (e.g. ÄPPELVINÄGER MED LINGON)
3 tbsp elderflower syrup (e.g. SAFT FLÄDER)
3 tbsp olive oil
Salt and black pepper

TO SERVE
4 portions bulgur
500 g broccoli
150 g feta cheese

1. Pre-heat the oven to 180°C.

2. Roast cherry tomatoes: Cut the tomatoes in halves or quarters depending on size. Place in an ovenproof dish. Mix the thyme, finely chopped garlic, olive oil, salt and pepper in a small bowl. Pour it over the tomatoes and mix well. Place the dish in the middle of the oven and cook for 20 minutes.

3. Place the frozen veggie balls onto a lightly oiled baking tray. Heat in the oven, below the tomatoes, for about 20 minutes.

4. Boil the bulgur as per the instructions on the packet.

5. Cut the broccoli into florets and boil for about 5 minutes or until still slightly al dente.

6. Elderflower vinaigrette: Mix all the ingredients together. Pour the vinaigrette over the broccoli and mix well.

7. Serve the veggie balls with bulgur, broccoli, pieces of feta and the roasted tomatoes.

Veggie balls in yellow curry
Serves 4

*Veggie balls are great in a spicy yellow curry. This is a good dinner
even without the accompaniments, but the lingonberry chutney and
fresh apple and cucumber salad add that something extra.*

32 veggie balls (e.g. GRÖNSAKSBULLAR)
Oil for frying

YELLOW CURRY MIX
1 large onion
2 cloves garlic
1 red chilli
2 tsp fresh ginger
2 tsp yellow curry powder
1 tsp cumin
2 tsp tomato purée
250 ml coconut milk
100 ml water
1 vegetable stock cube
Neutral oil for frying

APPLE AND CUCUMBER SALAD
2 apples
1 small cucumber
3 sprigs of mint
1 lime, juice of
Fresh coriander
Salt and black pepper

TO SERVE
4 portions jasmine rice
**4 pieces soft thin bread (e.g. BRÖD
    TUNNBRÖD)**
Lingonberry chutney, see p. 150

1. Boil the rice as per the instructions on the packet.

2. Yellow curry mix: Finely chop the onion, garlic and chilli. Grate the ginger. Heat the oil in a large saucepan and add the chopped ingredients and the ginger. Fry over a medium heat for about 5 minutes until the onion is soft and golden. Stir in the curry powder and cumin and fry for another 2-3 minutes. Stir in the tomato purée. Add the coconut milk, water and stock. Simmer for 10-12 minutes.

3. Fry the frozen veggie balls in oil for about 5 minutes until nicely browned. Place them in the sauce so they are hot when served.

4. Apple and cucumber salad: Cut the cucumber lengthways. Remove the watery middle and slice it and the apples. Place in a bowl with chopped mint, fresh coriander and lime juice.

5. Serve with jasmine rice, the apple and cucumber salad, lingonberry chutney and thin bread.

Meatballs in tomato sauce with aubergine
Serves 4

A good, filling meatball dinner with aubergine and tomato.
Unlike traditional polenta, instant or quick-cook polenta
is ready in a few minutes.

32 meatballs (e.g KÖTTBULLAR)
Oil for frying

TOMATO SAUCE
1 large aubergine
2 cloves garlic
1 onion
1 tin chopped tomatoes (400 g)
2 tsp vinegar (e.g. ÄPPELVINÄGER
　　MED LINGON)
approx. 1 tsp dried oregano
1 tsp sugar
Olive oil for frying
Salt and black pepper

INSTANT POLENTA
200 g instant polenta
approx. 30 g semi-hard cheese
　　(e.g. OST PRÄST) + some to garnish
approx. 1 tbsp butter
Fresh basil
Black pepper

1. Tomato sauce: Dice the aubergine. Heat a generous amount of olive oil in a large saucepan and fry the aubergine over a medium heat for about 10-15 minutes, or until the pieces are soft and golden brown all round. Chop the garlic and onion. Add to the aubergine pan along with the tomatoes, vinegar, oregano and sugar. Simmer for about 10 minutes. Season with salt and pepper.

2. Meatballs: Pre-heat the oven to 225°C. Place the frozen meatballs on a baking tray. Heat in the middle of the oven for about 15 minutes.

3. Instant polenta: Prepare as per the instructions on the packet. When done, add grated cheese and a knob of butter.

5. Place a large spoonful of polenta on the plate and add the meatballs and sauce.

6. Grate over a little cheese. Finish off with fresh basil and freshly ground black pepper.

Veggie balls with curry-fried cauliflower
Serves 4

Fresh herbs and curry give this main course plenty of flavour and colour. Instead of baking in the oven, the veggie balls can be fried in a large frying pan with the cauliflower if you prefer.

32 veggie balls (e.g. GRÖNSAKSBULLAR)
Oil for the baking tray

CURRY-FRIED CAULIFLOWER
1 head of cauliflower (approx. 500 g)
approx. 1/2 tsp yellow curry powder
Salt
Oil for frying

HERB POTATOES
600 g potatoes
1 clove garlic
3 tbsp parsley
2 tbsp chives
approx. 50 ml olive oil
Salt and black pepper

APPLE SALAD
2 apples
100 ml natural yoghurt, approx. 10 % fat

1. Boil the potatoes.

2. Pre-heat the oven to 180°C. Place the frozen veggie balls onto a lightly oiled baking tray and cook in the middle of the oven for about 20 minutes.

3. Curry-fried cauliflower: Remove the stem and slice the cauliflower. Rub in a little salt and yellow curry powder. Fry the slices in oil for a few minutes either side.

4. Herb potatoes: Finely chop the garlic and the fresh spices. Mix with the olive oil and fold in with the boiled potatoes. Season with salt and pepper.

5. Apple salad: Slice the apples. Mix with the yoghurt.

6. Serve the veggie balls with the curry-fried cauliflower, herb potatoes and apple salad.

Meatballs in spicy tomato sauce
Serves 4

Saffron, cumin and garlic spread wonderful aromas around the kitchen. You can add the meatballs to the sauce without frying to save time, but they won't have the same lovely colour.

32 meatballs (e.g. KÖTTBULLAR)
Oil for frying

TOMATO SAUCE
1 onion
2 cloves garlic
1 red chilli
1 tsp cumin
1 tsp mild paprika
1 tin chopped tomatoes (400 g)
1/2 g saffron
300 ml water
1 stock cube (vegetable or chicken)
approx. 1 tsp sugar
Olive oil for frying
Salt and black pepper

CARDAMOM COUSCOUS
4 portions of couscous
2 green cardamom pods
Salt

TO SERVE
100 ml natural yoghurt, approx. 10 % fat
Fresh mint

1. Chop the onion and fry over a medium heat in a saucepan until golden. Mix in the finely chopped garlic and chilli, and the cumin and paprika. Fry for a few minutes.

2. In another pan, fry the frozen meatballs in oil for about 5 minutes until nicely browned.

3. To the onion saucepan add the tomatoes, saffron, water and stock cube. Then add the warm meatballs.

4. Simmer the sauce for 10-15 minutes or so. Season with sugar, salt and pepper.

5. Cook the couscous as per the instructions on the packet, along with the cardamom and salt.

6. Serve the meatballs and tomato sauce with couscous, a dollop of yoghurt and a little fresh mint.

Chicken meatballs with roast root vegetables
Serves 4

An easy dish with Mediterranean flavours, and the oven does all the work. You can use normal potatoes instead of sweet, and carrots instead of parsnips.

32 chicken meatballs (e.g. KYCKLING-KÖTTBULLAR)
Oil for the baking tray

ROASTED ROOT VEGETABLES WITH HERB OIL
2 sweet potatoes
6–8 parsnips
2 cloves garlic
2 tbsp olive oil
2 tsp dried provençale spices (thyme, rosemary, oregano)
Salt and black pepper

TARRAGON YOGHURT
200 ml natural yoghurt, approx. 10 % fat
2 tsp dried tarragon
1 tsp runny honey
1 tsp Dijon mustard
Salt

TO SERVE
approx. 120 g mixed green salad

1. Pre-heat the oven to 225°C.

2. Roasted root vegetables with herb oil: Press the garlic into a bowl and mix with the oil, salt and spices. Cut the sweet potatoes and parsnips into sticks and place in an ovenproof dish. Pour over the herb oil and mix well. Cook in the oven for about 20 minutes.

3. When the root veg have about 15 minutes left, place the frozen chicken meatballs in an ovenproof dish. Put this underneath the root veg and heat the meatballs for about 15 minutes.

4. Tarragon yoghurt: Mix the yoghurt, tarragon, honey, mustard and salt in a bowl.

5. Place the green salad, sweet potatoes, parsnips and meatballs in large bowls.

6. Serve with a dollop of tarragon yoghurt.

Chicken meatballs with baked beetroot
Serves 4

A filling salad that makes a great main course. Instead of oranges you can use nectarines, pears or other seasonal fruits.på säsong.

32 chicken meatballs (e.g. KYCKLING-KÖTTBULLAR)
Oil for the baking tray

OVEN-BAKED BEETROOT
4 beetroots (450 g)
75 ml vinegar (e.g. ÄPPELVINÄGER MED LINGON)
3 tbsp lingonberry syrup (e.g. SAFT LINGON)
2 tbsp olive oil
Salt and black pepper

BLUE CHEESE SALAD WITH ORANGE
125 g blue cheese
80 g rocket
2 oranges
75 ml hazelnuts

DRESSING
1 shallot
Liquid from the beetroot

1. Oven-baked beetroot: Pre-heat the oven to 200°C. Peel the beetroots, cut into wedges and place in a small dish, e.g. a bread tin. Mix the vinegar, lingonberry syrup, olive oil, salt and pepper. Pour the mixture over the beetroot. Bake in the oven for about 45 minutes or until the beetroot is soft. Save the liquid for the dressing.

2. When the beetroot has been in the oven for around half an hour, place the frozen chicken meatballs in a lightly oiled oven dish and heat for about 15 minutes.

3. Blue cheese salad with orange: Toast the hazelnuts in a dry frying pan until they brown nicely. Cut nice fillets from the orange segments and put them in a bowl. Mix in pieces of blue cheese, rocket, toasted hazelnuts and baked beetroot.

4. Dressing: Mix the liquid from the beetroot with finely chopped shallot.

5. Serve the chicken meatballs with the blue cheese salad and dressing.

Chicken meatballs with chickpea salad
Serves 4

A filling salad that should be eaten warm. The chickpeas and chicken meatballs can be in the oven simultaneously. You can use chilli powder instead of paprika.

32 chicken meatballs (e.g. KYCKLING-KÖTTBULLAR)
Oil for the baking tray

CHICKPEA SALAD
1 tin chickpeas, drained (approx. 300 ml)
1/2 lemon, zest of
1 tbsp olive oil
1 tsp hot paprika
1 head of cauliflower (approx. 500 g)
80 g spinach
1 apple, hard and acidic
1 avocado
Salt and black pepper

DRESSING
1 tbsp whole-grain mustard (e.g. SENAP GROV)
1 tbsp elderflower syrup (e.g. SAFT FLÄDER)
1/2 lemon, juice of
4 tbsp olive oil
Salt and black pepper

1. Chickpea salad: Pre-heat the oven to 200°C. Put the chickpeas on one side of a baking tray. Mix with the lemon zest, olive oil, paprika, salt and pepper. Place the frozen chicken meatballs on the other side of the baking tray. Heat in the oven for about 15 minutes.

2. Remove the stem of the cauliflower and place the florets in a food processor a few at a time. Zap until the pieces are about the size of rice grains. If you don't have a food processor, use a grater. Cut the apple and avocado into wedges. Mix the chicken meatballs, chickpeas, cauliflower, spinach, sliced apple and avocado.

3. Dressing: Mix the mustard, elderflower syrup, lemon juice, oil, salt and pepper. Pour over the salad and mix well.

4. Dish up on plates to serve.

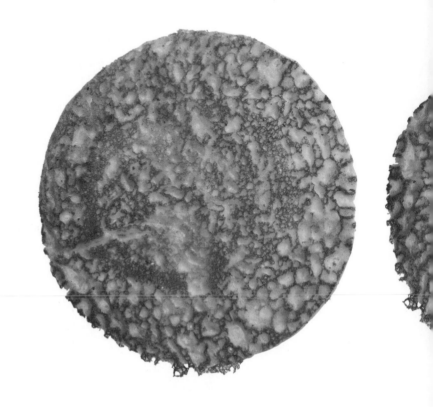

Pancakes

Pann

kakor

Pannkakor

PANCAKES... AND WAFFLES

Pancakes are probably one of only a few traditional Swedish foods that can be eaten as a starter, main course and dessert. Could be worth a try, so book out a day in your diary to get lost in the multifaceted world of pancakes. Pancakes have a good friend in pea soup. It's customary in Sweden to eat pea soup and pancakes on Thursdays. This is a tradition from the time when Sweden was a Catholic country and Friday was fasting day. But to make fasting a bit easier, people ate loads and loads on Thursday and topped it all off with loads and loads of pancakes. A kind of medieval 6:1 diet. Great!

Pancakes occur in one form or another in most cultures, but we think Sweden could be alone in its pancake gateau. It's a Swedish party classic that's particularly delicious in the summer. You'll find a classic pancake gateau recipe on page 108.

Basically the same mixture as for pancakes can be used to make small pancakes and waffles. Small pancakes are cute but they're a bit high maintenance – the babies of the pancake world, really – while waffles are the pancake's slightly more refined, cosmopolitan cousin.

Do you have eggs, milk, flour and butter at home? If so, what are you waiting for? Time for pancakes!

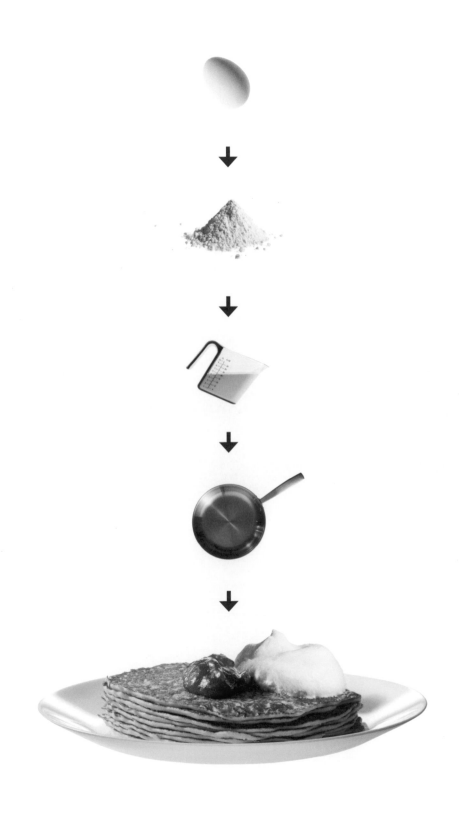

Pancake gateau

Serves 4

A great success for a Swedish party or a grand weekend breakfast.
A pancake gateau is the whole family's favourite.

12 pancakes (e.g. PANNKAKOR)

WITH JAM AND CREAM
**100 ml raspberry and blueberry jam
(e.g. SYLT HALLON & BLÅBÄR)**
**100 ml strawberry jam (e.g. SYLT
JORDGUBB)**
400 ml whipping cream
approx. 200 ml fresh berries, e.g. strawberries, blackberries, blueberries and
raspberries

WITH LEMON CREAM
300 ml whipping cream or quark
200 ml lemon curd
200 ml fresh berries to decorate

1. Pre-heat the oven to 200°C. Place the pancakes in an ovenproof dish and heat for about 15 minutes. Then leave to cool.

2. With jam and cream: Whip the cream. Layer pancakes, whipped cream and jam. Garnish with fresh berries.

3. With lemon cream: Whip the cream lightly. Add lemon curd and whip into a stiff cream. Layer pancakes and lemon cream. Garnish with fresh berries.

Tip:
Cream is easier to whip and grows bigger if it's really cold, around
5°C. If you're short on time, cool the cream in the freezer for about
20 minutes, but don't let it freeze.

Sweet pancakes
Serves 4

Delicious as a breakfast or snack, or a filling dessert.
You can also heat ready-made pancakes in a frying pan.

12 pancakes (e.g. PANNKAKOR)

COCONUT GRATIN
200 ml desiccated coconut
50 ml maple syrup
500 ml vanilla ice-cream

WITH CINNAMON-FRIED APPLES
2 apples
2 tbsp brown sugar
approx. 1 tsp cinnamon
approx. 3 tbsp butter

1. Coconut gratin: Pre-heat the oven to 200°C. Put the pancakes on a baking tray lined with baking paper. Sprinkle desiccated coconut and drizzle maple syrup over the pancakes. Bake for about 15 minutes. Serve with ice-cream and more maple syrup to taste.

2. With cinnamon-fried apples: Pre-heat the oven to 200°C. Place the pancakes in an ovenproof dish. Cut the apples into slices about 1.5 cm thick and turn in a mixture of brown sugar and cinnamon on a small plate. Place the slices on the pancakes along with a spoonful of butter. Bake in the oven for about 15 minutes. Serve with vanilla ice-cream.

Tip:
Leftover pancakes can be shredded and fried for a tasty snack.
Serve with lime sugar; see the recipe on p. 112 (under step 3).

Sweet waffles

Serves 4

Waffles make a delicious, appealing dessert or a luxurious breakfast. There are any number of variations, but here are some suggestions.

12 waffle hearts

CLOUDBERRY JAM AND CREAM
approx. 150 ml cloudberry jam
    (e.g. SYLT HJORTRON)
250 ml whipping cream

STRAWBERRIES WITH STEM GINGER
approx. 30 fresh strawberries
2 tbsp stem ginger
1 lime, peel of
Raw sugar

MASCARPONE, CHOCOLATE AND BANANA
100 ml chocolate spread
    (e.g. CHOKLADKROKANT BREDBAR)
100 ml mascarpone
approx. 30 blueberries
2 bananas
approx. 30 g dark chocolate,
    70 % cocoa

1. Pre-heat the oven to 220°C. Place the frozen waffles on a baking tray and heat for about 3 minutes.

2. Cloudberry jam and cream: Whip the cream. Put a spoonful of cream and cloudberry jam on each heart.

3. Strawberries with stem ginger: Slice or cut the strawberries. Mix with finely cut ginger. Grate the lime zest and mix with the raw sugar. Store in a jar. Place strawberries and stem ginger onto each waffle and sprinkle with lime sugar.

4. Mascarpone, chocolate and banana: Mix the chocolate spread and mascarpone. Put a spoonful on each waffle. Garnish with blueberries, sliced banana and chopped dark chocolate.

Savoury waffles

Serves 4

These lovely savoury bites make a great starter, snack or buffet dish.

12 waffle hearts

CAVIAR AND CRÈME FRAÎCHE
4 tbsp caviar (e.g. TÅNGKORN)
200 ml crème fraîche
1 red onion
Lemon
Black pepper

SHRIMP HASH
500 g shrimps, shells on
1 small red onion
4 tbsp chopped fresh dill + a little
    to garnish
100 ml mayonnaise
1/2 lemon, juice and zest
Salt and black pepper

GRAVLAX AND WASABI CREME
200 g gravlax
200 ml crème fraîche
1 tbsp wasabi
Dill
Black pepper

1. Pre-heat the oven to 220°C. Place the frozen waffles on a baking tray and heat for about 3 minutes.

2. Caviar and crème fraîche: Add a spoonful of caviar, crème fraîche and finely chopped red onion. Finish off with a slice of lemon and some black pepper.

3. Shrimp hash: Defrost and peel the shrimps. Place in a bowl. Mix in the chopped red onion, dill, mayo and lemon zest. Season with lemon juice and salt. Put a spoonful of the hash on each heart and garnish with some dill. Finish off with freshly ground black pepper.

4. Gravlax and wasabi creme: Mix the crème fraîche and wasabi. Place some wasabi creme and gravlax on each waffle. Garnish with a sprig of dill and a little black pepper.

Smör

Sandwiches

gåsar

smörgåsar

What would life be without sandwiches? Pretty dull. In Sweden the sandwich, which we often eat open, is a real everyday hero that saves all kinds of situations. Hungry? Have a sandwich. Dinner late? Have a sandwich. Missed lunch? Have a sandwich. A sandwich always tastes good, and can be topped or filled exactly the way you want. Go for something very quick and easy like just butter, or fancy it up with hot-smoked salmon and crème fraîche, topped with lemon and dill.

Sandwiches can be found in most cultures, and they come in all shapes and sizes. The American variety tends to have a lot more filling – and sometimes they're so big you really have to squeeze them together to fit them in your mouth! If you fancy trying a Vietnamese-inspired sandwich, why not turn to page 128 and make our version of banh mi with chicken meatballs?

Soft sandwiches are particularly good with soups, and crispbread with cheese and cucumber is a real Swedish classic. A sandwich can be made from crispbread, thin bread, white bread, rye bread and granary bread – pretty much any grain has a place in the sphere of sandwiches.

Getting hungry? Read on for some tips about how to vary out little everyday hero, the sandwich.

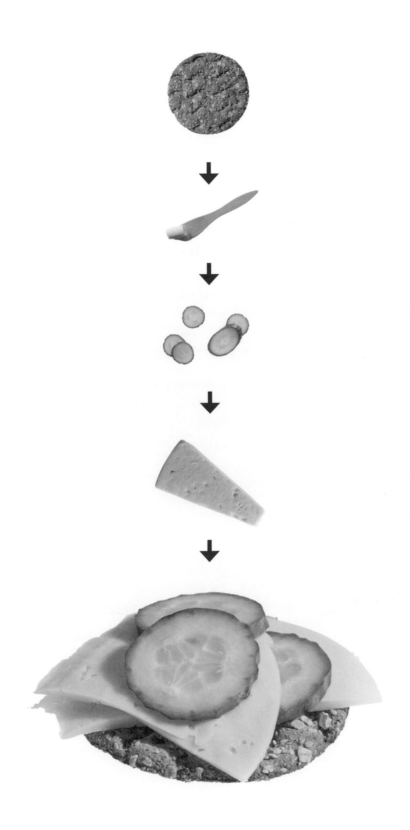

Crispbread variations
Serves 4

So humble and yet so tasty! Swedish crispbread comes in a wide range of varieties to go with everything from smoked salmon to blue cheese. Great anywhere, anytime.

RYE CRISPBREAD WITH SALMON RILLETTE

4 pieces of crispbread (e.g. KNÄCKE-BRÖD RÅG)

200 g hot-smoked salmon (e.g. LAX VARMRÖKT)

150 g cream cheese

1 lemon, zest of + approx. 2 tsp lemon juice

50 ml chives

2 ml cayenne pepper

Salt and black pepper

8 radishes

approx. 2 tbsp chives

MULTIGRAIN CRISPBREAD
WITH BLUE CHEESE

4 pieces of crispbread (e.g. KNÄCKE-BRÖD FLERKORN)

1 beetroot (cooked)

1 pear

approx. 70 g blue cheese

Butter

Sunflower shoots

1. Rye crispbread with salmon rillette: Mix together the cream cheese, finely grated lemon zest, lemon juice, chopped chives and cayenne pepper. Break off pieces of hot-smoked salmon and add them to the mix. Season with salt and pepper. Spread rillette onto each piece of crispbread. Garnish with sliced radish and chopped chives.

2. Multigrain crispbread with blue cheese: Butter the crispbread and add thin slices of beetroot and pear. Finish off with a piece of blue cheese. Garnish with sunflower shoots.

Shrimp and salmon sandwich with chive mayonnaise
Serves 4

A truly luxurious open sandwich featuring the delights of the sea.
Najad salmon or gravlax can be used instead of cold-smoked.

4 slices rye bread (e.g. made from BRÖDMIX FLERKORN)
500 g shrimps, shells on
200 g cold-smoked salmon

CHIVE MAYONNAISE
100 ml mayonnaise
2 tbsp chopped chives + a little to garnish

TO SERVE
approx. 40 g lamb's lettuce
4 tbsp caviar (e.g. TÅNGKORN)
Dill

1. Defrost and peel the shrimps.

2. Blend the mayo and chives with a stick blender.

3. Place the bread pieces onto a plate. Spread a layer of chive mayo onto each one and then add the lamb's lettuce, salmon and shrimps. Top with a spoonful of caviar, a few sprigs of dill, chives and an extra dollop of chive mayo.

Tip:
You can perk withered dill up by trimming a bit of the stem off and putting it in a glass of warm water in the fridge.

Gravlax sandwich with mustard sauce
Serves 4

IKEA's mustard and dill sauce has both sweetness and acidity, which really brings out the best in the salmon. This is a traditional Swedish starter that's also great as a lunch sandwich.

4 slices rye bread (e.g. made from BRÖDMIX FLERKORN)
200 g gravlax
approx. 2 tbsp butter
1 lemon
approx. 100 ml mustard sauce (e.g. SÅS SENAP & DILL)
Mixed green salad leaves
Dill
Black pepper

1. Spread each piece of bread with butter and add the salad leaves.

2. Place two slices of salmon on each sandwich and add a dollop of the sauce.

3. Serve with a slice of lemon and a sprig of dill.

Wrap variations
Serves 4

Blue cheese, BBQ chicken meatballs and cold-smoked salmon – here are three delicious lunch or picnic wraps.

4 pieces soft thin bread (e.g. BRÖD TUNNBRÖD)

BLUE CHEESE AND PEAR
125 g blue cheese
2 pears
approx. 2 tbsp sugar
approx. 80 g rocket
100 ml walnuts
Butter for frying

COLD-SMOKED SALMON AND HORSERADISH
400 g cold-smoked salmon
1 spring onion
1 head of cos lettuce
3 tbsp horseradish sauce
Cress

BBQ CHICKEN MEATBALLS
approx. 16 chicken meatballs (e.g KYCKLINGKÖTTBULLAR)
50 g blue cheese
approx. 100 ml BBQ sauce (smoky and sweet)
approx. 4 tbsp mayonnaise
4 carrots
1 stalk blanched celery
approx. 2 tbsp parsley

1. Blue cheese and pear: Slice the pears and roll them in sugar. Fry them quickly in butter. Fill the thin bread with cheese pieces, fried pear, rocket and walnuts.

2. Cold-smoked salmon and horseradish: Slice the spring onion and chop the lettuce. Mix with the horseradish sauce and salmon pieces in a bowl. Divide the filling between the four wraps. Garnish with cress.

3. BBQ chicken meatballs: Fry the chicken meatballs for 5 minutes or until heated through. Mix with the BBQ sauce. Coleslaw: Mix the blue cheese and mayo in a bowl. Slice the carrots and celery very thinly using, for example, a cheese slicer. Mix in with the cheese and mayo to make a coleslaw. Put some coleslaw, chicken meatballs and chopped parsley onto each piece of thin bread.

Banh mi with chicken meatballs
Serves 4

French-Vietnamese inspired baguettes with crispy quick-pickled vegetables. Sambal oelek gives the chilli mayo a real kick, but you can use any chilli paste.

4 baguettes
32 chicken meatballs (e.g. KYCKLING-KÖTTBULLAR)
approx. 2 tbsp sesame oil for the
    baking tray

CHILLI MAYONNAISE
100–150 ml mayonnaise
1–2 tbsp chilli paste, e.g. sambal oelek

PICKLED VEGETABLES
200 ml vinegar (e.g. ÄPPELVINÄGER MED LINGON)
100 ml water
2 tbsp sugar
1 ml salt
3 carrots (approx. 250 g)
2 red onions (approx. 150 g)

TO SERVE
approx. 4 tbsp fried onion (e.g. LÖK ROSTAD)
approx. 80 g rocket
Fresh coriander

1. Pre-heat the oven to 180°C.

2. Chilli mayonnaise: Mix the mayo and chilli paste. Set to one side.

3. Pickled vegetables: Mix together the ingredients for the pickling liquid. Stir until the sugar dissolves. Pour into a glass jar. Slice the carrots very thinly lengthways using, for example, a cheese slicer. Finely slice the red onion. Place the veg in the pickling jar and leave to stand until time to serve.

4. Place the chicken meatballs on a baking tray and drizzle on some sesame oil. Give the tray a shake to spread the oil nicely. Heat in the middle of the oven for about 20 minutes.

5. Cut the baguettes and remove some of the soft middle. Spread on a layer of chilli mayo, then add some rocket, chicken meatballs and pickled veg.

6. Garnish with the fried onion and fresh coriander.

Rye variations
Serves 4

Tasty, filling snack-time open Sandwiches that are best eaten with a knife and fork. Below is one sandwich base and two topping variations.

4 slices rye bread (e.g. made from BRÖDMIX FLERKORN)
2 tbsp whole-grain mustard
50 ml mayonnaise
Salt and black pepper

WITH VEGGIE BALLS AND CHERRY TOMATOES
approx. 8 veggie balls (e.g. GRÖN-SAKSBULLAR)
approx. 4 salad leaves
4 cherry tomatoes
1 small piece of cucumber
approx. 2 tbsp red onion

WITH MEATBALLS AND FRIED ONION
approx. 8 meatballs (e.g. KÖTTBULLAR)
1 onion
20 slices pickled gherkin (e.g. GURKA INLAGD)
approx. 2 tbsp fried onion (e.g. LÖK ROSTAD)
approx. 2 tbsp parsley
Butter for frying

1. Pre-heat the oven to 180°C. Place the meatballs or veggie balls in an ovenproof dish and heat in the middle of the oven for about 20 minutes.

2. Mix together the mustard, mayo, salt and pepper.

3. Veggie ball sandwich: Finely chop the red onion. Halve the cherry tomatoes and slice the cucumber.

4. Meatball sandwich: Finely slice the onion and fry in butter until soft. Season with salt and pepper.

5. Spread a layer of mustard mayo onto each sandwich. Add your choice of topping.

Shrimp sandwich with hard-boiled egg and mayonnaise

Serves 4

A snack or a small lunch sandwich when you fancy a little treat. IKEA shrimps are cooked when caught and then frozen, and are ready to eat once defrosted.

4 slices soft wheat bread (e.g. BRÖD MJUKKAKA)
1 kg shrimps, shells on
4 eggs
100 ml mayonnaise
2 tsp Japanese soy sauce

TO SERVE
1 head of cos lettuce
4 cherry tomatoes
1 spring onion
Dill

1. Defrost and peel the shrimps.

2. Hard boil the eggs. Peel and slice them.

3. Mix the mayo and soy sauce in a small bowl.

4. Spread a good layer of mayo on the bread. Add lettuce, shrimps, sliced egg and halves of cherry tomato.

5. Garnish with slices of spring onion and a sprig of dill.

Tip:
Defrost the shrimps quickly by putting them on newspaper and sprinkling a little salt over them.

Lin

Lingonberries

gon

LINGONBERRIES – ROBUST REBELS OF THE FOREST

Where nothing else grows or thrives, that's where you'll find the lingonberry. The berry's beautiful wintergreen shrub grows and breeds in our almost Arctic climate. Sweden's forests are full of the robust little lingonberries. And however much you pick, there's always more. A lot more. In fact, a long time ago it was decided in Sweden's parliament that there's enough lingonberries for everyone. Lingonberries paved the way for our famous 'allemansrätten', the public right of access, which means everyone is free to pick berries and mushrooms. Just think: millions of billions of lingonberries helped to create a democratic right for the people of Sweden and anyone who visits – what little rebels!

The acidic fresh berries aren't really that tasty, but quite bitter, almost sharp. But once you've acquired the taste, it's hard to live without them. A dollop of lingonberry jam or sugared lingonberries tastes great with meatballs or fried herring or pork or baked pancake or potato dumplings or black pudding or toad-in-the-hole. Check out our recipes and you'll see that they also work very well in everything from chutney to garam masala.

Are you ready for the robust red rebel of the forest? Great!

Lingon

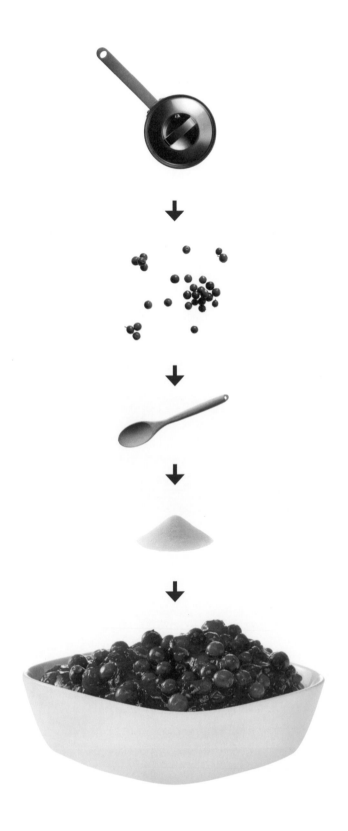

Muesli porridge with lingonberry jam
Serves 1

A filling, healthy Swedish breakfast with whole-grain oats, cran-berries and pumpkin seeds. This recipe adds an extra touch with spices, but it's great without them too.

150 ml muesli (e.g. MÜSLI MED TORKADE BÄR)
300 ml water
1 ml ground cinnamon
1/2 ml ground ginger
1/2 ml salt

TO SERVE
Lingonberry jam (e.g. SYLT LINGON)
Milk

1. Heat the muesli, water, spices and salt in a sauce-pan until it thickens into a porridge.

2. Pour into a breakfast bowl. Serve with lingonberry jam and milk.

Tip:
Lingonberry smoothie with muesli is another tasty snack or breakfast. Blend lingonberry jam, yoghurt and banana, and top with a little muesli. Using frozen banana makes the smoothie extra creamy and more like frozen yoghurt.

Lingonberry semifreddo with gingerbread
approx. 10 pieces

Semifreddo is an easy Italian ice-cream-like dessert. If you can't get fresh lingonberries, use some other nice berries to decorate. You can use sugar instead of honey if you like.

3 eggs
400 g lingonberry jam (e.g. SYLT LINGON)
50 ml runny honey
150 g gingerbread thins (e.g. PEPPAR-KAKOR)
300 ml whipping cream

TO SERVE
Fresh or frozen lingonberries

1. Separate the egg yolks and whites in two high-sided bowls.

2. Stir in the lingonberry jam, honey and crushed gingerbread thins into the bowl of egg yolks.

3. Whip the cream until stiff and stir into the egg yolk and lingonberry mix.

4. Beat the whites to a firm white foam. Fold carefully into the lingonberry mixture. The mix should retain as much air as possible.

7. Line a round springform cake tin, about 23 cm diameter, with cling film. Pour the mixture into the tin.

8. Freeze for at least 3 hours, preferably overnight. Remove from the tin a few minutes before serving. If the semifreddo won't come out, rinse the back of the tin with a little hot water.

9. Garnish with fresh lingonberries and cut into pieces.

Tip:
Try swapping regular ginger thins for ones with citrus (e.g. PEPPARKAKOR CITRUS) when you make the semifreddo.

Garam masala cake with lingonberry jam
10-12 pieces

Lingonberry jam, browned butter and warming spices give this cake a lot of flavour. Caster sugar can be used instead of brown sugar.

150 g butter
1 tsp cinnamon
1 tsp cardamom
1 tsp garam masala
3 eggs
300 ml brown sugar
100 ml lingonberry jam (e.g. SYLT LINGON)
300 ml plain flour
3 tsp baking powder
1/2 tsp salt
Butter for the tin
Breadcrumbs for the tin
Icing sugar to garnish

1. Pre-heat the oven to 175°C.

2. Grease and breadcrumb a loaf tin of about 1.3 litres.

3. Brown the butter in a saucepan over a medium heat. Stir and heat until golden brown. Stir in the cinnamon, cardamom and garam masala. Set aside to cool.

4. Whisk the eggs and brown sugar in a bowl until fluffy. Add lingonberry jam and the warm butter and spice mixture. Stir into a smooth mixture.

5. In another bowl mix the flour, baking powder and salt. Carefully fold into the mixture.

6. Pour the mixture into the tin and bake on the bottom shelf of the oven for about 45–60 minutes. Test the middle with a skewer. If it comes out dry, the cake is done.

7. Let the cake cool in the tin for about 10 minutes, before carefully turning it out onto a plate. Garnish with icing sugar once the cake has fully cooled.

Muesli and lingonberry flapjack
1 baking tray full

Really handy for a snack, these flapjacks are extra tasty dipped in a little dark chocolate. They have to be cooked long enough to be really crunchy, so don't take them out too soon. Suitable for freezing.

150 ml muesli (e.g. MÜSLI MED TORKADE BÄR)
100 ml brown sugar
2 tbsp warm water
50 ml neutral oil, e.g. sunflower oil
200 ml lingonberry jam (e.g. SYLT LINGON)
1 egg white
2 tsp cinnamon
1 tsp vanilla extract
1 tsp salt
200 ml desiccated coconut
200 ml any nuts

1. Pre-heat the oven to 125°C.

2. Dissolve the sugar in warm water in a bowl.

3. Mix in the oil, lingonberry jam, egg white, cinnamon, vanilla extract and salt.

4. Stir in the desiccated coconut, chopped nuts and muesli. Mix well.

5. Place baking paper on a baking tray. Spread the mixture out. Flatten until it's compact and about 1 cm thick.

6. Bake in the oven for about 70 minutes or until the mixture has set and the top is golden brown. Leave to cool.

7. Cut into squares and keep in an airtight container in the fridge.

Tip:
Nuts contain a lot of fat that can go rancid. Therefore keep these flapjacks in the fridge or freezer.

Chocolate cake with lingonberry jam
10-14 pieces

Acidic lingonberry and chocolate cream together on a chewy marzipan base. This easy gateau is perfect with a cup of coffee. Gluten and egg free.

**approx. 100 g marzipan
(e.g. MARSIPAN)**
Oil for the tin

FILLING
50 g butter
75 ml whipping cream
**200 g dark chocolate, 70% cocoa
approx. 150 ml lingonberry jam
(e.g. SYLT LINGON)**
Cocoa for garnish

1. Pre-heat the oven to 175°C.

2. Use a round springform cake tin, about 16 cm diameter. Line the base with baking paper and oil the inside edge.

3. Roll out the marzipan between two layers of cling film or baking paper so that it covers the base of the tin.

4. Place the rolled marzipan on the base, but not up the edge. Bake for about 8-10 minutes or until it colours nicely.

5. Filling: Melt the butter. Add the cream and bring to the boil. Remove from the heat and allow to cool slightly. Break up the chocolate and add. Stir until it has melted and you have a smooth mixture. Add the lingonberry jam. Pour the mixture into the tin and stand cold for at least 3-4 hours.

6. Garnish with sifted cocoa powder.

Lingonberry-steeped pears with marzipan sprinkles

Serves 4

A fast traditional dessert. You can prepare the pears in advance and keep refrigerated. The steeping liquid can be flavoured with a piece of fresh ginger or cinnamon stick.

300 ml lingonberry syrup (e.g. SAFT LINGON)
300 ml water
4 pears
approx. 150 g marzipan (e.g. MARSIPAN)
500 ml ready-made vanilla sauce (e.g. VANILJSÅS)

1. Bring the water and syrup to the boil in a saucepan. Peel the pears but leave the stalk. Cut the bottoms so they can stand on a plate.

2. Place the pears in the water and syrup mixture. Simmer with the lid on over a low heat for 10-20 minutes depending on how ripe the pears are.

3. Pre-heat the oven to 175°C. Grate or crumble the marzipan and place on a baking tray lined with baking paper. Roast for 3-5 minutes.

4. Remove the pears from the heat once they start to soften and leave to cool in the steeping liquid.

5. Serve with marzipan sprinkles, vanilla sauce and the steeping liquid.

Tip:
Ideally leave the pears cold in the steep for a day or so.
This enhances their colour and flavour.

Lingonberry chutney
approx. 400 ml

Chutney is used to enhance the flavour of all kinds of dishes.
Because a chutney should be acidic, sweet and rich, lingonberries
make the ideal base. Goes just as well with a plate of meatballs
as a cheese board.

400 g lingonberry jam (e.g. SYLT
  LINGON)
100 ml vinegar (e.g. ÄPPELVINÄGER
  MED LINGON)
1 clove of garlic, finely chopped
1 red onion
1 tsp cayenne pepper
Salt

VARIATION WITH SPICES
1 batch lingonberry chutney
1 tbsp fresh ginger, grated
1 cinnamon stick
1 tbsp yellow mustard seeds
Black pepper

VARIATION WITH SMOKY CHIPOTLE
1 batch lingonberry chutney
1 finely chopped chilli
2 ml chipotle
2 tsp butter

1. Bring the lingonberry jam to the boil in a pan
with the vinegar, finely chopped garlic, red onion
and cayenne pepper.

2. Add all the other ingredients except the salt
and pepper.

3. Simmer for about 30-40 minutes over a medium
heat. Stir occasionally to make sure the chutney
doesn't stick. It's ready when it thickens slightly,
and it will thicken more once it has cooled down.
Season with salt, and also a knob of butter for the
chipotle version.

4. Pour back into the jam jar and store in a cool place.

Tip:
Feel free to try other spices for the chutney such as
cardamom, cloves and orange peel.

Lingonberry loaf

2 loaves

An easy, juicy loaf that will keep for several days. It contains no yeast so there's no leaving it to rise, you can bake it straight away.

400 ml wholemeal flour
400 ml plain flour
300 ml oats + a little to garnish
200 ml mixed nuts
3 tsp bicarbonate of soda
2 tsp salt
2 tsp ground bread spice mix
1 L natural yoghurt
200 ml lingonberry jam (e.g. SYLT LINGON)

1. Pre-heat the oven to 175°C.

2. Mix all the dry ingredients in a bowl and add chopped nuts.

3. Pour the yoghurt and lingonberry jam over the flour mixture. Stir to ensure everything gets well mixed. The dough will be very sticky.

4. Line two loaf tins of about 1.3 litres with baking paper. Transfer the dough to the tins and sprinkle with oats.

5. Bake in the middle of the oven for about 60-75 minutes. Test the middle with a skewer. The loaves are ready when the skewer comes out dry.

6. Remove the loaves from the oven and leave to rest in the tins for about 15 minutes. Turn out onto a rack and leave to cool.

Tip:
These lingonberry loaves are great for freezing.
Freeze as fresh as possible, ideally slicing it first so you don't have to defrost a whole loaf every time.

Coffee time

Okay so we've called this section Coffee Time, but what we're really talking about is 'fika'. Fika is a very Swedish thing, and it's about more than just coffee really. More than coffee, but less than a proper meal. The ideal fika is a cup of good coffee with a sweet bun or a biscuit or a cake, or all three. But while the word fika is Swedish, coffee and something sweet is a phenomenon all over the world. Even so, Swedes are probably world leaders in eating buns, cakes and biscuits with their coffee. And fika break is deeply rooted in the essence of Swedishness. Fika break is where a group of workmates come together for 15 minutes or so over a cup of coffee with a biscuit or a cinnamon bun, for instance. Strengthened by caffeine and sugar, they then have renewed energy in their work. We're pretty sure that all good Swedish ideas and inventions were thought of just after a fika break.

So when you fika – yes, it's a verb as well – you ideally have a bun or a piece of cake or a biscuit with your coffee. But to do it properly, you should really have seven types of sweet thing with it. That was certainly the rule in the old days. If you offered people less than seven, you were considered mean, and if you offered more it was a sign of vanity.

We've skipped the more everyday varieties and come up with eight (oops!) new ones of our own. Happy dunking!

Jam biscuits

Makes approx. 30

*These shortbread biscuits are a Swedish classic. Also try
flavouring them with lemon zest and cardamom.*

200 g butter, room temperature
150 ml sugar
1 egg yolk
400 ml plain flour
1 tsp baking powder
1 tsp vanilla extract
1 ml salt
**approx. 100-150 ml jam (e.g. SYLT
KRUSBÄR, SYLT JORDGUBB or SYLT
HALLON & BLÅBÄR)**

1. Pre-heat the oven to 160°C.

2. Beat the butter and sugar in a bowl until light and fluffy.

3. Add the egg yolk.

4. Mix the flour, baking powder and salt. Carefully fold into the mixture and add the vanilla extract. Don't stir unnecessarily.

5. Shape the dough into a roll about 4 cm in diameter, and wrap in cling film. Leave to stand cold for about 30 minutes.

6. Cut the dough into slices 1 cm thick. Make a pit in the middle with your thumb or a teaspoon. Put about a teaspoon of jam on each biscuit. Put them on a baking tray lined with baking paper and bake for 14-16 minutes or until golden brown.

Tip:
*Biscuits stored in a tin with a sugar cube
will stay crunchy for longer.*

Elderflower and lemon drizzle cake
10-12 pieces

*A lovely fresh cake that tastes of summer. Perfect for making
a day before serving as it only gets moister overnight.*

250 ml sugar
2 eggs
250 ml natural yoghurt
150 ml neutral oil, e.g. sunflower oil
2 lemons, zest of
500 ml plain flour
1 1/2 tsp bicarbonate of soda
Oil for the tin

ELDERFLOWER AND LEMON SYRUP
**150 ml elderflower syrup (e.g. SAFT
    FLÄDER)**
50 ml sugar
1–2 lemons, juice of (50 ml)

1. Pre-heat the oven to 175°C.

2. Use a round springform cake tin, about 23 cm diameter, and line the base with baking paper. Oil the inside edges.

3. Whisk the sugar and eggs until light and fluffy, then add the yoghurt, oil and finely grated lemon zest.

4. Mix the flour and bicarbonate of soda in a bowl. Carefully fold into the mixture. Don't stir unnecessarily.

5. Pour the mixture into the tin and bake for about 45-50 minutes. Test the middle with a skewer. When the skewer comes out dry, the cake is done.

6. Heat the elderflower syrup and sugar in a saucepan. Stir until the sugar dissolves. Pour in the lemon juice.

7. Make small holes all over the cake with a skewer while it's still hot. Drizzle over the elderflower and lemon syrup. Leave to stand in the tin for about 15 minutes. Take the cake out, place on a rack and leave to cool.

Butterscotch cookies with sea salt
Makes approx. 30

The sea salt contrasts with the sweet and enhances the chocolate flavour of these easy, slightly chewy cookies. Take care not to cook for too long or they'll go hard.

100 ml chocolate spread
   (e.g. CHOKLADKROKANT BREDBAR)
250 ml plain flour
50 ml cocoa powder
150 ml sugar
1 egg
100 g dark chocolate, 70 % cocoa
Sea salt

1. Pre-heat the oven to 160°C.

2. Mix the chocolate spread, flour, cocoa, sugar, egg and finely chopped chocolate in a bowl.

3. Roll the cookie dough into balls and leave to stand cold for about 30 minutes.

4. Place baking paper on a baking tray. Put the balls on the tray and flatten them a little. Bake for about 11-14 minutes. Remove from the oven and sprinkle on a little sea salt.

5. Store in a glass jar.

Tip:
Chocolate should be stored in a cool, dark place but not in the fridge.

Chewy marzipan and coconut biscuits
Makes approx. 25

Almond and coconut make these biscuits nice and moist.
Don't make them too high or they may bake unevenly.

200 g marzipan (e.g. MARSIPAN)
600 ml desiccated coconut (200 g)
50 g butter, room temperature
2 medium eggs
50 ml sugar
1 ml salt
1 tsp vanilla extract

VARIATION WITH CHOCOLATE
50 g dark chocolate, 70 % cocoa

1. Pre-heat the oven to 175°C.

2. Grate the marzipan.

3. Mix all the ingredients together.

4. Place baking paper on a tray. Put small heaps of dough on the tray using two spoons, or by hand.

5. Bake in the middle of the oven for about 15 minutes or until they've browned nicely. Remove from the oven and leave to cool.

Variation with chocolate: Melt the chocolate, drizzle it over the cookies and leave to harden.

Banana cake with dark chocolate
10-12 pieces

This cake pays tribute to the unbeatable combination of banana and chocolate. The riper the bananas, the more flavoursome the cake.

150 g butter
2 eggs
100 ml natural yoghurt
3 bananas
100 g dark chocolate, 70 % cocoa
400 ml plain flour
250 ml sugar
2 tsp baking powder
1 tsp vanilla extract
Butter for the tin
Breadcrumbs for the tin

1. Pre-heat the oven to 175°C.

2. Grease and breadcrumb a loaf tin of about 1.3 litres.

3. Brown the butter over a medium heat, stirring all the time, until it starts going golden brown. Remove from the heat and allow to cool slightly.

4. Whisk the eggs and yoghurt in a bowl. Add the mashed bananas and chopped chocolate. When the butter has cooled slightly, add it to the egg mixture.

5. Mix the flour, sugar and baking powder in a bowl. Fold into the egg mixture without stirring too much. Add the vanilla extract.

6. Pour the mixture into the tin and bake for about 50 minutes. Test the middle with a skewer. The cake is ready when the skewer comes out dry.

7. Let the cake rest in its tin for about 10 minutes, then turn onto a rack to cool.

Tip:
Never keep bananas in the fridge,
it turns them black.

Cinnamon crunch

This recipe turns leftover sweet buns into cinnamon crunch, which makes a great present. You can make similar kinds of crunch from any wheat-based sweet bread.

As many leftover cinnamon buns as you like

1. Pre-heat the oven to 150°C.

2. Cut the buns into slices about 1-1 1/2 cm thick. Place on a baking tray.

3. Dry in the oven for about 30 minutes. Remove from the oven and leave to cool.

4. Store in a glass jar.

Swedish apple sponge with vanilla sauce
10-12 pieces

*This delicious cake will quickly become a favourite. You can swap
the apples for a different seasonal fruit.*

3 apples

3 eggs

200 g marzipan (e.g. MARSIPAN)

200 ml sugar

150 ml neutral oil

300 ml plain flour

3 tsp baking powder

1 tsp vanilla extract

1 ml salt

2 tsp ground cardamom

1 tsp ground ginger

Oil for the tin

TO SERVE

**500 ml ready-made vanilla sauce
(e.g. VANILJSÅS)**

1. Pre-heat the oven to 175°C.

2. Peel and slice the apples.

3. Use a round springform cake tin, about 23 cm diameter. Line the base with baking paper and oil the inside edge.

4. Beat the eggs and sugar until light and fluffy.

5. Grate the marzipan and stir it into the egg mixture along with the oil.

6. Mix the flour, baking powder, salt and spices in a bowl. Carefully fold the flour mixture into the egg mixture. Add the vanilla extract. Transfer to the tin.

7. Carefully push the apple slices down into the cake mixture.

8. Bake in the middle of the oven for 60-65 minutes. Test the middle with a skewer. The cake is ready when the skewer comes out dry. Leave to stand in the tin for about 10 minutes. Turn out onto a rack.

9. Serve cold or warm with vanilla sauce.

*Tip:
Apples keep best in the fridge. Bear in mind that
apples secrete a substance that makes other fruit
and vegetables ripen faster.*

Brownies with crumbled cookies

approx. 20 servings

Sticky treats with a strong chocolate flavour.
Crumbled oat crisps provide a crunchy contrast.

200 g dark chocolate, 70 % cocoa
200 g butter
4 eggs
300 ml sugar
2 tsp vanilla extract
150 ml plain flour
12 oat crisps (e.g. KAKOR HAVREFLARN)

1. Pre-heat the oven to 175°C. Line an ovenproof dish about 32 x 22 cm with baking paper.

2. Melt the butter and chocolate in a pan over a very low heat. Remove from the heat and stir in the eggs, sugar, vanilla extract and flour.

3. Pour the mixture into the tin. Break the oat crisps into bits over the mixture and push in lightly.

4. Bake for about 25 minutes. The cake should still be sticky but not runny. Leave it to cool.

5. Cut the cake into squares.

Tip:
For more classic brownies, replace the
crumbled cookies with hazelnuts.

smorgasbord

Imagine a big table full of all the tasty food you can imagine. There you have the basic idea behind a Swedish smorgasbord. The name comes from 'smörgås' meaning sandwich, and 'bord' meaning table. But it's not really about sandwiches, it's about variety. You'll find everything from hot dishes to marinated herring, from omelettes and gratin dishes to bakes. Help yourself to cold cuts of meat, smoked salmon and plump, golden brown meatballs. A smorgasbord is often a pretty protein-rich affair. Yes you'll see a few boiled potatoes, but otherwise vegetables are dazzlingly absent from this classic Swedish buffet.

If you're making your own smorgasbord, remember that variety is the spice of life. The level of ambition is up to you. You can put on a standard buffet with a few tasty dishes like marinated herring, salmon and meatballs. Or you can be inspired by our recipes and present a fine salmon bake, a magnificent pickled herring cake and meatballs with an exciting lingonberry chutney, along with gorgeously crunchy crispbread and a nice salad. Mix wildly and let your guests choose what they want! Come on now – please all help yourselves!

Smör gås bord

Smorgasbord

Here we've laid out a smorgasbord with a selection of the dishes in this book. We've also added some ready-made products and accompaniments that you just have to present on plates, bowls and dishes. Think of our smorgasbord as an inspirational guide and put together your own buffet depending on how you feel, what you fancy and how much time you have.

The great thing about a smorgasbord is that once you've put everything out, the rest takes care of itself.

178

1. Mustard-tossed potatoes

Recipe on page 58. Potato salad that's just as good cold as warm. You can make the mustard dressing up to two days in advance.

2. Pickled cucumber

Recipe on page 84. Can be made in advance. Leave to stand in the fridge and take out an hour or so before serving.

3. Mustard sauce (e.g. SÅS SENAP & DILL)

The perfect sauce for gravlax or cold-smoked salmon.

4. Chocolate cake with lingonberry jam

Recipe on page 146. Ideally make the cake the day before serving. Cover with cling film and leave to stand in the fridge until time to serve. Garnish with cocoa powder.

5. Three kinds of bread

Thin bread, rye bread and crispbread. Crisp-bread can be put out in advance. Put the soft bread out just before serving.

6. Three kinds of cheese

Ost Herrgård (semi-hard), Ost Präst (semi-hard) and Ost Blåmögel (blue). Take the cheese out of the fridge and stand at room temperature for a few hours before serving.

7. Salmon bake

Recipe on page 26. Can be prepared in oven dishes the day before and cooked for 1-2 hours before the guests arrive.

8. Waffle hearts with gravlax and wasabi creme

Recipe on page 114. Cook the waffles in plenty of time before the party so they have time to cool down.

9. Herring tapas

Recipe on page 26. The curry cream can be made a day in advance, but only put it on the crispbread just before serving or the crispbread will go soft. The potatoes can be roasted several hours in advance.

10. Lingonberry chutney

Recipe on page 150. Ideally make the chutney several days beforehand.

11. Veggie balls and meatballs

Prepare as per the instructions on the packet.

12. Three kinds of salmon

Gravlax, hot-smoked and cold-smoked. The salmon can be put onto serving dishes in advance. Cover with cling film and leave to stand in the fridge until time to serve.

13. Pickled herring cake

Recipe on page 16. Ideally make the cake the day before. Cling film the dish and leave to stand in the fridge. Garnish just before serving.

Cocktails

Here are some festive alcohol-free drinks. Use a shaker to make mixing easy and also look professional, but you can also stir the ingredients straight in the glass or carafe. Each recipe makes one serving. If you're using them as a meal-time drink, dilute with more water and decorate with frozen berries and sliced fruit.

Alcohol-free mojito

30 ml syrup (e.g. SAFT FLÄDER, SAFT LINGON or SAFT RABARBER)
1/2 lime
approx. 10 mint leaves
Fizzy water
Ice

MINT-FREE VERSION
Replace the mint with frozen raspberries and apple slices

1. Use a cocktail muddler to crush the mint and lime wedges in a glass. Add the juice and fill up the glass with ice. Mix and top up with fizzy water. Decorate with mint leaves and a lime wedge. Makes about 180 ml.

Blueberry cocktail with cinnamon

50 ml blueberry syrup (e.g. SAFT BLÅBÄR)
80 ml water
20 ml pressed lemon juice
1 ml vanilla extract
approx. 1 ml cinnamon + a little to garnish
Ice

1. Mix the blueberry syrup, water, lemon juice, vanilla extract, cinnamon and ice in a glass, or shake them all in a cocktail shaker. Remove the ice cubes or sieve the drink. Garnish with a little more cinnamon. Makes about 150 ml.

Spicy rhubarb cocktail

approx. 1 cm slice of red chilli
40 ml rhubarb syrup (e.g. SAFT RABARBER)
approx. 1 tsp ginger syrup
1/2 lime, juice of (approx. 1 tbsp)
150 ml fizzy water
Ice

GINGER SYRUP
1 1/2 tbsp chopped fresh ginger
200 ml water
100 ml sugar

1. Ginger syrup: Bring the water, ginger and sugar to the boil and simmer for about 10 minutes. Sieve, pour into a bottle and stand in a cool place. This syrup is great for all kinds of drinks and will keep for several weeks in the fridge.

2. Crush the chilli with a cocktail muddler in a glass. Pour over the rhubarb syrup, ginger syrup and pressed lime. Fill up with ice. Mix and top up with fizzy water. Makes about 200 ml.

Elderflower cocktail with cucumber

approx. 3 cm cucumber
30 ml elderflower syrup (e.g. SAFT FLÄDER)
20 ml lemon juice
80 ml water
Ice

1. Muddle or blend the cucumber. Mix the liquid with ice, elderflower syrup and lemon juice. Shake or stir. Sieve and pour into a glass, and fill with water. Makes about 150 ml.

Lingonberry cocktail with grapefruit

40 ml lingonberry syrup (e.g. SAFT LINGON)
approx. 80 ml freshly pressed grapefruit juice
80 ml water
Ice

1. Mix the lingonberry syrup with the pressed fresh grapefruit in a glass. Add ice and top up with fizzy water.

Warm rosehip cocktail

250 ml rosehip drink (e.g. DRYCK NYPON)
1 tsp vanilla extract
1/2 cinnamon stick
2 cardamom pods (or 2 ml coarse-ground cardamom)
2 tsp chopped fresh ginger

1. Mix all the ingredients in a saucepan and bring to the boil. Reduce the heat and simmer, covered, for about 7-10 minutes. Sieve and pour into a large glass. Makes a great dessert cocktail and can also be served with ice-cream or whipped cream. Makes about 200 ml.

Find the food

Soft wheat bread
BRÖD MJUKKAKA
Gravlax with poached egg and
herb oil 66
Shrimp sandwich with hard-boiled
egg and mayonnaise 132

Thin bread
BRÖD TUNNBRÖD
Butter, cheese & herring 14
Veggie balls in yellow curry 90
Veggie balls with tabbouleh 86
Wrap variations 126

Cheese

Blue cheese
OST BLÅMÖGEL
Chicken meatballs with baked
beetroot 100
Crispbread variations 120
Wrap variations 126

Herrgård semi-hard cheese
OST HERRGÅRD
Butter, cheese and pickled
herring 14
Cold-smoked salmon with brussels
sprout salad 72
Smoky chilli salmon and salad with
pan-toasted corn 76

Präst semi-hard cheese
OST PRÄST
Fried salmon with cauliflower
purée 62
Lemon risotto with cold-smoked
salmon 28
Meatballs in tomato sauce with
aubergine 92
Najad salmon with baked egg 32
Salmon and kale salad with
lemon 68

Salmon with potato & fennel
gratin 56

Chocolate & marzipan

Chocolate spread
CHOKLADKROKANT BREDBAR
Butterscotch cookies with sea
salt 162
Sweet waffles 112

Dark chocolate, 70% cocoa
CHOKLAD MÖRK 70 %
Banana cake with dark
chocolate 166
Brownies with crumbled cookies 172
Butterscotch cookies with sea
salt 162
Chocolate cake with lingonberry
jam 146
Sweet waffles 112

Marzipan
MARSIPAN
Chewy marzipan and coconut
biscuits 164
Chocolate cake with lingonberry
jam 146
Lingonberry-steeped pears with
marzipan sprinkles 148
Swedish apple sponge with vanilla
sauce 170

Easy to prepare

Chicken meatballs
KYCKLINGKÖTTBULLAR
Banh mi with chicken meatballs 128
Chicken meatballs with baked
beetroot 100
Chicken meatballs with chickpea
salad 102

Chicken meatballs with roast root
vegetables 98
Wrap variations 126

Mashed potatoes
POTATISMOS
Swedish meatball platter 84

Meatballs
KÖTTBULLAR
Meatballs in spicy tomato sauce 96
Meatballs in tomato sauce with
aubergine 92
Rye variations 130
Swedish meatball platter 84

Pancakes
PANNKAKOR
Pancake gateau 108
Sweet pancakes 110

Veggie balls
GRÖNSAKSBULLAR
Rye variations 130
Veggie balls in yellow curry 90
Veggie balls with curry-fried
cauliflower 94
Veggie balls with roast cherry
tomatoes 88
Veggie balls with tabbouleh 86

Waffle hearts
VÅFFLOR
Savoury waffles 114
Sweet waffles 112

Fish & seafood

Caviar
TÅNGKORN
Savoury waffles 114
Shrimp and salmon sandwich with
chive mayonnaise 122

Find the food

Cold-smoked salmon
LAX KALLRÖKT
Cold-smoked salmon bake 26
Shrimp and salmon sandwich with chive mayonnaise 122
Wrap variations 126

Cold-smoked salmon fillet
LAX KALLRÖKT FILÉ
Cold-smoked salmon with brussels sprout salad 72
Cold-smoked salmon with preserved vegetables 78
Lemon risotto with cold-smoked salmon 28

Gravlax
LAX GRAVAD
Gravlax sandwich with mustard sauce 124
Gravlax with poached egg and herb oil 66
Savoury waffles 114

Hot-smoked salmon
LAX VARMRÖKT
Crispbread variations 120
Hot-smoked salmon salad with pear vinaigrette 64
Salmon and potato fry with caviar sauce 52
Tagliatelle with hot-smoked salmon and gremolata 36

Marinated herring
SILL DILL, SILL INLAGD, SILL SENAP
Herring tapas 20

Najad salmon
LAX NAJAD
Najad salmon with baked egg 32

Pickled herring
SILL MATJES
Butter, cheese and pickled herring 14
Herring tapas 20
Pickled herring cake 16
Pickled herring, egg and potatoes 18

Salmon fillet
LAX FILÉ
Bibimbap with salmon and fried egg 70
Fried salmon with cauliflower purée 62
Salmon and kale salad with lemon 68
Salmon burger with celery coleslaw 54
Salmon fishcakes and mango salsa 74
Salmon parcels with vegetables 42
Salmon soup with green curry 30
Salmon soup with saffron and thyme aioli 44
Salmon tartare with chilli and lime 34
Salmon with potato & fennel gratin 56
Salmon with red cabbage salad 58
Salmon with summer vegetables and lemon sauce 60
Salmon with sweet potato & lentil salad 40
Salmon with teriyaki sauce and pak choi 46
Sesame-coated salmon with noodle salad 50
Smoky chilli salmon and salad with pan-toasted corn 76
Tandoori-spiced salmon with fennel raita 48

Shrimps, shells on
RÄKOR MED SKAL
Salmon soup with saffron and thyme
  aioli 44
Savoury waffles 114
Shrimp and salmon sandwich with
  chive mayonnaise 122
Shrimp sandwich with hard-boiled
  egg and mayonnaise 132

Side of salmon
LAX HELSIDA
Salt-baked salmon with potato
  & beetroot salad 38

Sauces, jams & condiments

Cloudberry jam
SYLT HJORTRON
Sweet waffles 112

Cream sauce
GRÄDDSÅS
Swedish meatball platter 84

Fried onion
ROSTAD LÖK
Banh mi with chicken meatballs 128
Rye variations 130
Salmon tartare with chilli and
  lime 34

Gooseberry jam
SYLT KRUSBÄR
Jam biscuits 158

Horseradish sauce
SÅS PEPPARROT
Salmon burger with celery
  coleslaw 54
Salmon with red cabbage salad 58
Wrap variations 126

Lemon and dill sauce
SÅS CITRON & DILL
Salmon with summer vegetables
  and lemon sauce 60

Lingonberry jam
SYLT LINGON
Chocolate cake with lingonberry
  jam 146
Cold-smoked salmon with brussels
  sprout salad 72
Garam masala cake with lingon-
  berry jam 142
Lingonberry chutney 150
Lingonberry loaf 152
Lingonberry semifreddo with ging-
  erbread 140
Muesli and lingonberry flapjack 144
Muesli porridge with lingonberry
  jam 138
Swedish meatball platter 84

Mustard sauce
SÅS SENAP & DILL
Gravlax sandwich with mustard
  sauce 124

Pickled cucumber
GURKA INLAGD
Rye variations 130

Raspberry and blueberry jam
SYLT HALLON & BLÅBÄR
Jam biscuits 158
Pancake gateau 108

Strawberry jam
SYLT JORDGUBB
Jam biscuits 158
Pancake gateau 108

Vanilla sauce
VANILJSÅS
Lingonberry-steeped pears with
  marzipan sprinkles 148

Swedish apple sponge with vanilla
  sauce 170

Vinegar
ÄPPELVINÄGER MED LINGON
Banh mi with chicken meatballs 128
Bibimbap with salmon and fried
  egg 70
Chicken meatballs with baked
  beetroot 100
Cold-smoked salmon with brussels
  sprout salad 72
Cold-smoked salmon with
  preserved vegetables 78
Fried salmon with cauliflower
  purée 62
Hot-smoked salmon salad with pear
  vinaigrette 64
Lingonberry chutney 150
Meatballs in tomato sauce with
  aubergine 92
Salmon with red cabbage salad 58
Salmon with sweet potato & lentil
  salad 40
Salmon with teriyaki sauce and pak
  choi 46
Salt-baked salmon with potato
  & beetroot salad 38
Sesame-coated salmon with noodle
  salad 50
Veggie balls with roast cherry
  tomatoes 88

Whole-grain mustard
SENAP GROV
Chicken meatballs with chickpea
  salad 102
Cold-smoked salmon with
  preserved vegetables 78
Rye variations 130
Salmon with red cabbage salad 58

PRODUCTS YOU CAN FIND AT IKEA

The main ingredients in all the recipes can be found at most IKEA stores. However, products may of course run out or our range may change for reasons beyond our control. If you have any food allergies or intolerances, please carefully check the ingredients of any items you are planning to buy from IKEA. IKEA accepts no liability for any allergic reactions that may occur. The other ingredients in this book can be found in most well-stocked supermarkets. Please consider the environment and choose organic where possible.

THANK YOU!

Thanks to everyone in the work group! You wouldn't believe how we've fried Salmone, tasted sauces, burnt Salmone, photographed, acquired new Salmone, washed up pots and pans, looked for green enough limes, eaten our fill and had such a laugh.

Here at IKEA we aim to provide as much inspiration as possible, but with minimal impact on the environment. In accordance with our sustainability strategy "People and Planet Positive", our books take the environment into account in every stage of production, from the choice of paper to how we distribute our printed material. The book you are holding is printed on paper that meets all the requirements for responsible forestry. This means, for example, that the paper raw material comes from trees that are certified to originate from a sustainably managed forest. We print using vegetable-based printing inks without solvents. Read more about how IKEA is working for a sustainable future at www.IKEA.com.